D0083342

26-6443   HQ1784   88-29784 CIP
Arab Women's Solidarity Association Conference. (1st: 1986: Cairo, Egypt).
**Women of the Arab world: the coming challenge: papers of the Arab
Women's Solidarity Association Conference**, ed. by Nahid Toubia; tr. by
Nahed El Gamal.   Zed Books (Dist. by Humanities) 1988.   168p index **ISBN
0-86232-784-9, $45.00; ISBN 0-86232-785-7 pbk, $15.00**
      The first publication and translation into English of writings by members of
the Arab Women's Solidarity Association (AWSA). The Association represents an
ambitious attempt to unite leading feminists from the entire Arab world. This collection, comprising the proceedings of AWSA's first conference, reflects pan-Arab
focus and concerns. Nawal Saadawi places contemporary Arab feminism in context, and warns of two dangers. The first is nationalist insistence that feminists
must wait for their country's problems to be solved before they advance their own
agenda (articles on Palestinian women's roles in the West Bank and in Gaza under-
score her argument). The second is degradation of women by fundamentalists under the guise of honoring them (see Fouad Zakaria's article). Fatima Mernissi
analyzes the Arab notion of time as resolutely anachronistic and concludes that
the women's movements threaten the need for stasis. Iqbal Baraka deals with the
influence of male writers on the women's movements, contrasting the profeminist
stands of 19th-century thinkers with the misogyny of 20th-century writers. There
are also interesting articles on women's work and health. Unlike *Women in the
Muslim World*, ed. by Lois Beck and Nikki Keddie (CH, Mar '79), Elizabeth
Fernea's *Women and the Family in the Middle East* (1985), and Nadia Hijab's
Womanpower (CH, Jan '89), this collection is written for Arab women. For libraries at all levels with women's studies holdings.—*M. Cooke, Duke University*

Women of the Arab World
The Coming Challenge

Women of the Arab World
The Coming Challenge

**Papers of the
Arab Women's Solidarity Association
Conference**

Edited by Nahid Toubia
Translated by Nahed El Gamal

Zed Books Ltd
London and New Jersey

Women of the Arab World: The Coming Challenge
was first published by
Zed Books Ltd., 57 Caledonian Road, London N1 9BU, UK and
171 First Avenue, Atlantic Highlands, New Jersey 07716, USA,
in 1988

Copyright © Arab Women's Solidarity Association 1988

Typeset by EMS Photosetters, Rochford, Essex
Cover designed by Lee Robinson
Printed and bound in the United Kingdom at
The Bath Press, Avon

British Library Cataloguing in Publication Data

Women of the Arab world: the coming challenge:
  papers of the Arab Women's Solidarity
  Association.
  1. Arab countries. Women. Social conditions
  I. Toubia, Nahid   II. Arab Women's
    Solidarity Association
  305.4'2'09174927

  ISBN 0-86232-784-9
  ISBN 0-86232-785-7 Pbk

DEDICATION

To every Arab woman who possesses the courage to strive for change, for a better quality of life, for greater exactitude in the exercise of justice and wider horizons of freedom, we dedicate this first book in the series of publications of the Arab Women's Solidarity Association.

Nawal El Saadawi

Contents

Tables

Foreword

It is fortunate to be born to witness the age of feminism, and then asked to help introduce the pioneer feminist work written by a group of Arab women. This book is a selection of papers, presented at the first Arab Women's Solidarity Association Conference held in Cairo, in September 1986. It was not the first conference to be held in the name of women in Arab countries, but this one was different. I would like here to present my personal experience as a testimony to a new generation of women in the Middle East.

I first became aware of my rejection of conventional values on women at the age of seven. Was it related to the birth of my baby brother? Perhaps. There was a seed of rebellion in me as there is in hundreds and thousands of women in Egypt and the Arab world. Despite the apparent extreme social oppression of women, the seed grew; maybe due to a relatively healthier, basically egalitarian atmosphere at home. There was also constant nourishment from the examples of brave and capable women encountered in my daily life: a teacher at primary school, a street vendor, our widowed neighbour, my unmarried aunt, my biology and English teachers, among many others. These women may not have had a chance to say 'No', but still were able to stand tall and brave, carving an independent path for themselves in a male-dominated world.

Then came the feminist movement of the 1970s. I was again lucky to be middle class and educated and able to utilize a colonial heritage of having mastered an international language; I immersed myself in the wealth of literature; it said what I had been feeling for years. The examples were different from my own immediate reality but the concepts were the same. Shortly afterwards came Nawal El Saadawi's books, public lectures and debates, bringing the truth nearer home and eliminating the psychological barrier of being an imported movement.

I felt personally saved but what of all those women around me? How can the few of us pass on the message? For over ten years nothing significant happened in the women's scene in the region. We remained isolated, alienated individuals, engaged in reinforcing our own islands. Then came the idea of the Arab Women's Solidarity Association, as Nawal explains in her introductory chapter; and, on 1 September 1986, the dream became a reality. Now in my mid-thirties, I thought I had lost the ability to feel the joy and freedom of new discoveries. But to be in the same hall with hundreds of women from my own culture, speaking the same language, was indeed a rejuvenating experience. We came from different political backgrounds, had different methods of analysis and variable personal choices, but we were one. We were together in our aspiration for freedom as women.

The difference this time was the feminist character of the Conference – feminism not as revolutionary indoctrination, academic theory or even an ideology. Feminism may have a multitude of definitions, encompassing the choices of women of all colours and social groups throughout the world, provided there is a choice.

To me, feminism is foremost a 'feeling' – of which I am not ashamed. It is the state when women no longer suppress their feelings of anger and love, of rage and ecstasy, of revenge and beauty. It is when women feel free to use their immense emotional energy to explore and redefine their position in the world. It is when they use their intellect and wit, education and skills, and their rich heritage of knowledge and wisdom to redesign their role in the past, present and future of humanity. Feminism is the fire that melts, but does not destroy.

The chapters in this book provide an insight into the minds and the creative consciences of some Arab feminists. It is not a complete picture of the reality of all Arab women today, but it is a beginning. All the participants are intellectual, middle-class, urban women, but many may have a rural and/or poor background. The papers range from the philosophically contemplative, the statistically precise to first-hand personal experiences. There is a wide variety of political thought represented, including liberal feminist and classical Marxist. The authors are from seven different Arab countries while the Conference participants were from 14 countries. The one contribution from a man, Dr Fuad Zakaria, reflects the Association's policy of not excluding those men who stand in solidarity with our struggle, and the importance of Dr Zakaria's thoughts as a progressive Islamic thinker on the current hot issue of Islamic fundamentalism.

The papers speak for themselves, but I would like to direct the reader to the important views of the Palestinian women living in the occupied lands: Mona Rishmawi, Rita Giacaman, Mona Oda. Of particular importance is Dr Mona Rishmawi's well-documented and argued paper on the laws under which Palestinian women live in the so-called Israeli democracy. It is evidence of the breaches of human rights perpetrated by the Israeli government which are now apparent to the whole world through their reactions to the mass uprisings in the occupied territories.

We are making our voices heard. May the world stop to listen.

Nahid Toubia
Khartoum, March 1988

Introduction

Nawal El Saadawi

The Arab Women's Solidarity Association

The idea of establishing the Arab Women's Solidarity Association was born with the 1970s. The idea emerged as a group of free-thinking Arab women became increasingly aware of and alarmed by the forms of subjugation suffered by Arab women and Arab peoples in general. The truth dawned upon us that the liberation of Arab peoples will never be accomplished unless women are liberated, while the liberation of women is by necessity dependent on the liberation of the land as well as liberation from economic, cultural and media domination. We firmly believed that solidarity was the only means to consolidate our power, for right without power is ineffective, weak and easily lost.

The solidarity of Arab women became a hope we exchanged whenever we met on any territory. We held a number of preparatory meetings in Egypt, Lebanon, Kuwait, Tunisia, Syria, Jordan, Morocco, the Sudan, Algeria, Yemen, and so on. In 1982, the foundations of the Association were laid. We applied for, and in 1985 were granted, consultative status with the Economic and Social Council of the United Nations as an Arab non-governmental organization. This organization was to be international, non-profit making, and aimed at the promotion of Arab women and Arab society in general, politically, economically, socially and culturally – and sought to consolidate the ties between women in all Arab countries.

Since 1982 a large number of Arab women, both those living in the Arab area and abroad, have joined the Association. The following years, however, witnessed a set-back for the rights women had acquired during the 1950s and 1960s. The fierce attack launched against women was but an integral part of the siege that (despite apparent differences in their attitudes) neo-colonialism, Zionism and Arab reactionaries laid against the Arab nation to stifle its voice and end its struggle for independence. Despite the involvement of religious fundamentalist movements in several battles against Israel and against Western influence, they have been hostile to the cause of women, because of their reactionary attitude towards democratic, social and even basic national issues.

It has become evident that many of the traditional standpoints adopted on issues related to Arab women and their rights are in opposition to the true development of Arab societies. The present situation calls for a deeper, more modern look into the role of women, both in society and the family, and for a clearer definition of the objectives of the Arab women's movement in its task of enhancing freedom and exacting justice for the millions of Arab citizens whose yoke is not easy.

General objectives of the Association

The main principles and objectives of the Association may be summarized as follows:

Women's active participation in the political, social, economic and cultural life of the Arab countries is a prerequisite for the exercise of democracy.

For the institution of social justice in the family and at the national level, all forms of discrimination on the basis of sex both in public and private spheres should be eliminated.

Guided by a scientific approach and an enlightened mind, efforts should be made, in a spirit of understanding of the real needs of women in the contemporary Arab environment, to promote the creative development of women and the emergence of their distinctive personality to enable them to criticize the ideas and values aimed at undermining their struggle for freedom.

To combine intellectual and practical endeavours in order to improve work conditions and the general quality of Arab women's lives and to take substantive and continuous steps to reach the broadest sectors of women in the poorer classes both in rural and urban areas.

To participate actively in projects aimed at intensifying the participation of women in political, economic, social and cultural activities at private and public levels; to explain to women the relationship between their problems and the problems of the society at large; and to open new fields of activities for the creative endeavours of women for the liberation of the mind and the stimulation of the capabilities of youth.

To open membership of the Association to those men who believe that advancement of Arab society cannot be accomplished without the liberation of women.

Difficulties encountered

Under the present conditions of dissent and fragmentation within the Arab nation, the establishment of an association for the solidarity of Arab women was no easy task.

Arab women are dominated by men in every area of life in the patriarchal family system: state, political party, trade union and public and private institutions of all types. It is not surprising, therefore, that the problems of Arab societies all reflect on the solidarity of Arab women.

Despite these difficulties, we have succeeded in drawing a large membership of Arab and Egyptian women who believe in their cause. We have also succeeded in registering the branch in Egypt after the Ministry of Social Affairs (as the competent body to approve the registration) had refused our application on the pretext that the State Security Police and the Criminal Control Department were opposed to the idea. Following support for our campaign by prominent writers and public figures inlcuding Fathy Radwan, Mustafa Amin and Salah Hafez, on 7 January 1985 the Arab Women's Solidarity Association was officially registered and came into being.

Activities of the Association

The Association has participated in a number of activities for Arab women held at the local and international levels.

In 1985, it sent a delegation to the International Conference on Women in Nairobi, where it organized a seminar on Arab women and social values to which valuable studies were presented. Our delegation took part in the meetings and marches organized by Arab women during the Conference and the Association presented a Statement by Arab Women's Solidarity Association (see Appendix 1) which was circulated as one of the Conference documents.

The Association took part in the campaign launched against the set-back to the position of women precipitated by the modification of the Personal Status Law of Egypt in 1985. In addition to holding meetings and issuing statements, the Association submitted proposed modifications to the draft law to the People's Assembly.

Cultural seminars on the issue of women were held during the period 1982–87. During the first week of April 1985 the Association also invited the Black American writer Angela Davies to Egypt. The programme of her visit included several meetings with a number of prominent women leaders in Egypt.

The Association played a significant role in raising public awareness of the danger of certain drugs used as contraceptives. The Minister of Health was approached on the matter, articles were published by members and an urgent appeal was addressed to the Medical Syndicate.

The Conference

As the Conference was conceived as a social and cultural as well as a scientific assembly, invitations were not restricted to academic specialists alone. The aim was to achieve a large gathering of Arab women to pledge solidarity and closer ties. Invitations were also addressed to certain men noted for their interest in the cause of women and the liberation of Arab thought.

The majority of the studies presented to the Conference on the Challenges Confronting Arab Women at the End of the 20th Century, held in Cairo from 1 to 3 September 1986, are contained in this book. The studies were discussed in plenary sessions and in four committees: the political, economic, social and cultural committees. The resolutions and recommendations resulting from its deliberations are set out in Chapter 16. The inaugural session was attended by 159 participants from various Arab countries.

The Conference may be said to have realized its three basic objectives, namely:

1. To study the challenges confronting Arab women at the end of the 20th century in the political, cultural, economic and social fields.

2. To establish an assembly of a large number of Arab women intent on solidarity and co-operation to become an effective force for the liberation of themselves and of their Arab societies.

3. To convene the general assembly of the Association; to elect its board of directors and its representatives to the United Nations; to modify certain of its statutory articles; and to approve projects for the forthcoming period.

The city of Cairo was chosen as a venue for the Conference in view of its distinctive position in the Arab world, and its being the location of the Arab Women's Solidarity Association. The Arab League premises were to house the Conference to emphasize Arab solidarity in the face of neo-colonialism and Zionism, as well as of the reactionary and fanatic movements pervading the Arab world in recent years which direct their blows particularly at women. Women, it should be noted, are the perennial and essential victims of all attacks launched against movements for the liberation of peoples and movements for the institution of human rights.

Preparations for the Conference took a year and a half. Having decided to hold the Conference in Cairo, we applied to the Ministry of Social Affairs for its approval, but received no reply. We then applied to the Ministry of Foreign Affairs, the competent authority for matters concerning Arab and international organizations, the Association being an Arab international organization with consultative status with the UN Economic and Social Council. Our application was approved, and appended to it was a courtesy note from Foreign Minister Dr Esmat Abdel Meguid. The efforts of Mrs Mervat El Tillawi, Minister Plenipotentiary at the Egyptian Foreign Ministry, deserve special mention.

Financial difficulties
Confronted by the lack of funds for the Conference (our resources consisted of the annual subscription fees of 10 Egyptian pounds per member) the Association approached certain Arab and Egyptian organizations for contributions. None of these proposed the funding, or responded to our request – even long after the deadline; the Association, therefore, had no choice but to approach certain international organizations in Egypt. Of those approached by the head of the preparatory committee, OXFAM and the Ford

Foundation in Cairo responded positively. Their contributions, though not very large, were unconditional, and on these grounds were accepted by the Association as being in conformity with its statutes. Later, we also received small contributions from certain international organizations concerned with women, but the main funding was provided by NOVIB in Holland.

The contributions we received covered the expenses incurred by a large number of researchers and Association members from various Arab countries who were invited to the Conference, there being no conditions attached to the funding apart from the understanding that it be used for Conference purposes.

Conference emblem

The Conference adopted the emblem of the Association: 'The Power of Women – Solidarity – Lifting the Veil from the Mind'. It appears on all the Association's letterheads and publications, and on the invitation cards for the Conference. The emblem is envisaged to combine the basic objectives of the Association, namely solidarity, without which women cannot become a power, and awareness, which necessitates the lifting of the veil. It was conceived to have the largest appeal possible, drawing women from different political and conceptual trends, political parties, governments, trade unions, non-governmental organizations, etc., for how can anybody object to solidarity or to the freedom to think and exercise the powers of the mind?

Success of the Conference

The assembly halls of the Arab League headquarters witnessed for the first time a gathering of Arab women representing no government or party, and the walls resounded with the vigour and enthusiasm of a younger generation. During the three days of the Conference, the four committees reviewed 24 studies; women's books on art and literature were on display. Coverage of the Conference was undertaken by Egyptian, Arab and international media, a fact which brought many issues of a conceptual nature to the forefront. Some attempts were made by certain political movements to influence the course of deliberations and to attack the Conference as well as the Association, but these failed.

Attitudes of certain political movements towards the Conference

Islamic 'salafi' movements

Most of these boycotted the Conference from the beginning, considering that the emblem 'Lifting the Veil from the Mind' and 'Solidarity of Arab Women' to be a transgression of God's commands and a violation of religious law. Consequently they rejected the invitation and prohibited their female members from attending. Nevertheless, a number of women Islamic thinkers endowed with independent minds participated actively in the deliberations of the Conference. Newspapers published by the Islamic fundamentalist movements made numerous and diverse charges against us, the least of which were infidelity and atheism. We were also charged with treason for having accepted Conference funding from non-Islamic and non-Arab sources.

Traditional rightist movements

These too, boycotted the Conference from the very start. For them, the Arab Women's Solidarity Association is a communist organization because we associate the domination of women as a class with partriarchal domination. The word 'class' is totally banned from the usage of such political movements. For them, we should assume the role of a women's charitable society to care for the sick and those with war disabilities, doing little more than distributing sweets. Political issues, historical perspectives or class conflict as they reflect on women are all domains into which we should never enter. In this context, traditional rightist movements said we were communists recruited by the Soviet Union to serve its interests.

Traditional leftist movements

These accused us of being agents of the USA and Zionism for having accepted a grant from the Ford Foundation. When these charges failed to produce the desired effect, however, we were attacked from another direction. The ideas put forward and discussed were said to separate the cause of women from that of the nation, or were concerned with the sexual aspect only and neglected the political and economic aspects, or were dividing the ranks by antagonizing men, and so on.

The government

The Ministry of Social Affairs completely ignored the Conference by not responding to our invitation. Some members of the government press attacked the Conference and pressured the authorities to inspect the Association's records. The Ministry of Foreign Affairs, however, adopted a positive attitude by approving the convening of the Conference and making possible the booking of the necessary facilities of the Arab League premises.

The crisis of democracy and the press

The articles sent to national and opposition newspapers in answer to the attacks and charges heaped on the Association were for the main part refused publication. The few articles which were eventually published were meddled with in one way or another, with sections deleted or titles changed. In spite of the fact that Egyptian law provides for the right to reply in the same newspaper, on the same page and in the same space, we were, without exception, denied this right by all newspapers in Egypt.

This situation, however, should cause no surprise because for the press, as in politics, 'might makes right'. In the world of the media, rights are taken, never granted.

The very first draft resolution adopted by the Association at its latest general assembly held on 1 September 1986 called for the establishment of a publishing house and the issue of a newspaper or magazine to propagate the views of the Association. This book is the first fruit.

Arab Women's Solidarity Association, Cairo
January 1987

1. The Political Challenges Facing Arab Women at the End of the 20th Century*

Nawal El Saadawi

The simple truth which escapes people's thinking

A woman who had received an invitation to attend one of the discussion sessions organized by the Women's Solidarity Association contacted me. She is a university teacher, who wanted to participate in the session. Her husband, however, had refused, forbidding her to leave the house. This is a man who believes that work outside the home is not only a woman's right, but indeed her duty, in order to elevate the financial and social level of her family. He sees no justification, however, for a woman to leave her home for any other purpose. His wife had explained to him the importance of her attendance at this meeting, and had said that she wanted to achieve a greater understanding of the major problems facing women specifically and to participate with other women in solving them. He was not convinced, and told her that women have no problems – for after all, they have acquired education and gained employment as professors, government ministers, doctors, and engineers. So, then, what can their problems be?

After the couple had discussed the matter at length, the husband threatened his wife with divorce, should she leave the house in order to attend the session.

This sort of incident recurs frequently in the lives of most Arab women from all sectors of the population. Women may practise their rights by making personal decisions to be active in public life – thereby sacrificing their married lives. Or they may prefer the security of marriage to public activity in the political and cultural spheres. A man may divorce his wife if she goes against his orders; even if he does not divorce her, the spectre of divorce hovers, a sword of Damocles, over her head.

In Egypt and in most of the other Arab countries, men no longer reject the notion that a woman has the right to work outside the home.[1] In most cases, however, men do reject women's participation in public political or cultural activities.

In some Arab countries, the law stipulates explicitly that a man has the right to prevent a woman from going outside the home without his permission. In

* Trans. by Marilyn Booth.

other cases, while there is no explicit statement to this effect, a man is given the right to prevent a woman from going out to work if this conflicts with the welfare of the family; and it is the man who defines what is the welfare of the family.

How, then, can we talk about the political challenges facing the Arab woman without being aware of this obstacle which prevents her participation in political activities – an obstacle that men do not face?

In all countries of the Arab region, if a man decides to participate in a public discussion group, a political party, or any other political or cultural activity, no one threatens him with divorce, or prevents him from leaving the house.

This is an extremely simple fact, yet it is one not readily present in people's minds. It reveals to us the strong and organic mutual link between the public political challenges facing an Arab woman and the private family-related challenges which she must meet, simultaneously, if she wants to play a role in political life – or even hold a view independent of her husband's. This challenge faces all women, of all classes and sectors, from poor women in rural areas to upper-class women, including the wives of the nations' rulers and presidents.[2]

The public, political challenges and the private, individual challenges in the life of an Arab woman cannot be separated, and she cannot confront one without facing the other as well.

This is a clear and scientifically established fact – but it is missing from most existing political studies on Arab women. Most researchers in this field, both women and men, separate political from family life. They see women as independent beings who must practise their political rights, such as the right to be nominated and elected to the People's Assembly or the National Assembly. Thus, in such studies, a complete dissociation is made between the woman and the family, as if the woman is the one who makes decisions concerning her movements and activity outside the home, without a father, a brother, or a husband who possesses authority over her.

A constitutional chasm

The constitutions of most Arab countries state that all citizens are equal in their public rights and duties, and stipulate that people are equal before the law. For example, Article 40 of the Egyptian Constitution of 1971 states: 'Citizens are equal before the law; they are equal in public rights and duties, with no discrimination made on the basis of race, sex,* language, religion, ideology or belief.'

Reading this constitutional Article quickly, one might believe that the Constitution stipulates equality between women and men. But a careful reading reveals that this equality is only true of public rights and duties. This is the fundamental chasm found in the constitutions of the Arab nations; the

* In Arabic, the word *jins*, conveying the basic meaning of 'kind' or 'category', can refer to both sex and race. (Trans.)

division between public and private, from which oppression and exploitation of women are derived and maintained. The Constitution makes a distinction between a person's public political rights and duties and her/his private rights and duties.

Is a person divided into two parts – a public one and a private one? Does a person become a different person merely by entering the home? Is not the family the kernel of society, or does it exist in another society, or another world?

We know that this chasm, this separation between 'public' and 'private', was established solely to subjugate women to man's control, and to impose duties upon them without giving them rights. It was created to conceal the contradiction between their public duties towards the state and their duties within the family.

This contradiction is revealed when we see that labour laws give women equal rights to work as men, but that women cannot actually practise this right because of marriage laws – for it is a woman's husband, not she, who possesses the right to make decisions in this matter.

Thus, in the Arab nations, women are under the authority of two, contradictory laws. The first is a public law which does not distinguish between citizens on the basis of sex or religion, and gives them human and civil rights – hence the right to work, the right of freedom of movement and other human rights. The moment the woman crosses the threshold of her home, she is ruled by another law, based on division and distinction according to sex and religion.

The contradiction appears clearly also in this text from the 1971 Egyptian Constitution: 'The state guarantees a balance and accord between a woman's duties towards her family, on the one hand, and towards her work in society, and her equality with man in the political, social, and cultural spheres, on the other, without violating the laws of the Islamic Shari'a.'

This constitutional text clarifies the following:

1. A woman is delegated two duties of work, inside the home and outside it. First, her ancient obligation towards the family and, second, her new one towards society.

2. No new rights are awarded to the woman inside the family based on her new duties towards society.

3. Men are not delegated new obligations towards their families in return for the new duties that women are expected to assume in society.

4. It is stipulated that the laws of the Islamic *sharia* may not be compromised in situations of equality between women and men in public rights and duties.

Thus, we discover that even in public rights and duties, the equality between men and women in the Constitution is made conditional, and is constantly threatened as different interpretations of the Islamic *sharia* arise. This is the only article in the Constitution which lays down this condition.

Discrimination on the basis of sex and gender has not been effaced

The justice of the law depends fundamentally on its application to all people regardless of race or sex, religious belief or class.

The basis on which the public laws are constructed are those that give the individual status as a citizen of his country who has a particular national identity. However, the foundation of the laws concerning individual behaviour – the Personal Status Laws – is the individual's status as a member of a particular sex and a certain religious belief.

Thus, this second group of laws lacks the most fundamental criterion of justice and is constructed upon the division made between people on the basis of religion and sex. According to the rational definition of justice, such laws would be considered racist, just as the racist laws of South Africa and Israel distinguish between people on the basis of religion and race.

The peoples of Africa, Asia and South America, currently labelled 'the Third World', have been able to acquire and represent a growing strength in the United Nations; they have succeeded in making accusations against these kinds of racist governments and in revealing the international forces which support them. Women have participated in this struggle just as men have. Women's liberation movements all over the world[3] have played their role in creating pressure and influence, to the extent that the United Nations designated 1975–1985 as the Decade of Women, in which all forms of distinction based on sex and gender would be terminated.

Such efforts, made over the past few years, resulted in the United Nations Covenant of 19 December 1979 that outlaws all forms of prejudice against women and which, by the end of 1985, had been signed by 171 nations. The Covenant establishes that women and men must share authority equally in the nation and in the family. Article 16 stipulates the wife's equality with her husband in all rights and duties within the family and outside it.

It is a strange paradox that some of the Arab nations which have signed this Covenant announce in their reports to the United Nations that equality between men and women has been achieved, even though the reality we can observe confirms that the distinction remains, maintained in the laws concerning marriage and the family, as well as in the public or civil laws and in the Constitution.

The schizophrenia in laws and values

From the moment our Arab nations were subjected to traditional colonialism, the public or civil laws in our countries were changed to safeguard the imperialist interests of the colonialist – economic, commercial, security-related and political.

Colonialists were not concerned with changing the Personal Status Laws in the colonies. This was the standard policy – to interfere only in changing the laws which touch upon their immediate interests, and thereby guarantee quick profits from the various production sectors. This emphasis on fast profits necessitated a level of modernization and development in the public or civil laws to facilitate the active movement of trade.

No immediate interests were involved in the development of the Personal Status Laws. Indeed, the opposite was true. It was in the interests of colonialists and their supporters in local governments to maintain the status quo – and maintain the discrimination between people on the basis of religion, race, or sex.

Britain and France were among the most deeply rooted imperialist nations in our Arab region, and as a consequence they were among the nations most concerned to preserve existing distinctions between different categories of people and to maintain racial and religious laws which could spark off sectarian division when necessary. They aimed to create a schizophrenic split in the laws, in order to modernize some sectors of the society at the cost of others, to open the upper classes to the civilization of the West, and to lock the overwhelming majority – especially the rural population – into the ancient heritage.

The neo-colonialists followed the path of the old,[4] and this division in laws and values came to prevail in our nations. There are the public or civil laws, which are constantly being changed according to what is needed to facilitate the speed of production of goods and services, and to encourage consumption. And there are the family laws which sow in people's inner selves a passive indifference, an attitude of submission, a tendency to resort to the past or to spiritual powers to solve their financial crises.

This schizophrenia is reflected in political and social life, just as it is mirrored in moral and cultural life. In the sphere of economics and politics, we see the contradiction clearly in the civil (autocratic) rules which rely on religious (theocratic) laws. These systems submit to commercial rules which impose women's nudity in advertisements for consumer goods (including tourist goods and services) while the religious laws impose the veiling of women.

We see an opening up to the petrodollar and the technology of video and pornographic films, together with a mental locking of doors to embrace only the past and our predecessors. We see absolutist, pyramidal systems of rule, and a forced unity of opinion, which refuses to accept diversity except in the sphere of polygamy. We see capitalist styles of development in tribal desert societies, be they nomadic or agricultural. We see a vast wealth, derived from oil, scattered throughout foreign banks and hotels at the same time as the majority of the Arab peoples are suffering from poverty, illiteracy, physical and social malaise. We see a modernization of utter superficiality – in which millions are spent on importing luxury goods or on restoring an ancient stone dome, in the midst of peoples who are deprived of basic necessities.[5]

The Arab women suffers most from these contradictions; she is the first victim of this schizophrenia, and it is on her body that the contradiction materialises. She hides her hair beneath a thick head-veil while revealing her waistline under a snugly fitted belt, and abandons her higher education to become a fashion model in a show of garments for veiled women. She becomes the mannequin of the late 20th century.[6]

It has become common to see the dignified religious scholar speaking on television about the importance of veiling women, to be followed immediately by a half-naked dancer singing a commercial advertisement for American shampoo.

The Arab woman is the sacrificial lamb in the political arena

It goes without saying that a law cannot be changed without political or military force. Rights are lost without the possibility of power, whether on state or individual levels.

The state that has military power is not bound by the decisions of the United Nations or the International Court of Justice. How often has the government of Israel, or of South Africa, been condemned for its violations of international law, the United Nations Charter, and the decisions of the Security Council? Yet such a condemnation is never transformed into a true punishment of the offending government.

Within a society, no oppressed group can win its rights and change the laws for its own welfare unless it has political or military power. Leaving aside the question of military force – for this is an undemocratic power based on violence, in addition to being limited to men – only access to political power will enable Arab women to change public or private laws to make them more just, less schizophrenic, and less contradictory.

But this political power has not yet been realized for women in any Arab nation to this day. Despite the increase in the number of women with high levels of education, women professionals, and those distinguished by their work in various labour unions and professional associations, political parties and parliaments, Arab women are still a marginal minority, not exceeding 8%, in all of these political organizations.[7]

The laws of all of the Arab nations still do not allow women to form a political force. All they permit is the establishment of charitable or cultural associations that make it possible for women to be active socially in a limited fashion, and on the condition that they do not become politically active except in government-sanctioned spheres.

I remember, in 1985 – when Egyptian women lost some of their rights through the abolition of Personal Status Law No. 44 (1979) – the Arab Women's Solidarity Association became active in the popular women's movement which demanded a new law that would be more just. (The Egyptian branch of the Arab Women's Solidarity Association, incidentally, is registered with the Ministry of Social Affairs as a community association.)

I was astonished when I received a threat from the authorities in the Ministry of Social Affairs. When I inquired about the reason, I was told that 'the Law of Association prohibits political activity.' I said, 'Our activity does not go beyond the demand for changes in the law governing marriage and divorce,' to which they replied, 'This is political activity. Don't you know that any attempt to change any laws is political activity?'

I knew this in theory, but there is a great difference between theoretical knowledge and experience. In most Arab nations women had obtained what were called 'political rights' – that is, the right to the vote, nomination and election to parliament. But this experience proves that the acquisition of this right has not transformed women into a political force able to put pressure and change the laws to their benefit.

The marriage and divorce laws have been changed in a number of Arab countries since mid-century, and women have obtained partial and minor rights. But these changes resulted less from women's political power than from struggles and balances or reconciliations between other political forces.

The best example of this happened in Egypt in 1985, when a judgement of unconstitutionality was issued concerning Personal Status Law No. 44 (1979); it was replaced by Law No. 100 (1985).[8] Let us read what the Center for Political and Strategic Studies, al-Ahram, Cairo, said about that law in a political report issued in 1986:

> In spite of the fact that the court's ruling [on the abolition of the 1977 Personal Status Law] was based on formal legalities concerning the manner in which the law was issued rather than its contents, the Islamic movement succeeded in its propaganda in placing the spotlight on the law's contents. In this, it was backed by most ruling and oppositional religious and political experts. The contents include articles considered to be closer in position to a liberal view on women's rights than to the conservative Muslim position on this issue. The government and parliament responded to this campaign, and resumed discussion of the contents of the law. The result was a law which comes closer to the demands of the Islamic movement.

This is how the Egyptian woman in 1985 lost some of her rights merely because there was a desire on the part of other political forces, governmental and oppositional, to placate the conservative Islamic forces. Such incidents are happening throughout the Arab countries – and thus the woman has become the sacrificial lamb of the political sphere.[9]

The contradictions amongst the progressive political forces

The political sphere in the Arab world is witnessing a new struggle for power amongst a number of conflicting political groupings, one of them being the conservative religious forces. The struggle is concentrated around the ruling structure of the state, the interpretation of the concepts of succession and counsel [*Succession* of one ruler to another by delegation or choice of new ruler by *Counsel* of elders; two forms of government advocated by Islam. (Ed.)], and the way in which authority and wealth are distributed. The conservative religious forces regard religion and the state as inseparable, and they believe that all the laws, whether governing public or private matters, must have a religious basis.

Secularist political forces regard the separation of religion and state as a fundamental necessity. They believe that the laws should be based on a concept of civil law, in which Personal Status Law has no place. But these latter forces either keep completely quiet or they agree with the religious forces, in considering the Personal Status Law as a religious law which must conform to the rulings of the *sharia*. And thus the contradiction exists, despite the secularist progressive outlook of these groups.

One misapprehension of the relatively progressive political forces in the Arab countries is that they can win the struggle against the conservative religious groups by backing down or compromising in some areas, especially on the question of women's rights. They do not realize that when the conservative forces gain grounds in these important mass issues, such gains will strengthen their position and create leverage for them to move on more successfully to the rest of the issues.

In a discussion session on Islam and secularism (on 11 July 1986, in Cairo), the secularist side defended the importance of separating civil laws from religion without mentioning the Personal Status Law. This silence was maintained despite the fact that the conservative religious side spoke at great length on this subject, stressing the importance of making women submissive to men within the family, veiling them, and distancing them from public life – to protect morals, prevent social mixing of the sexes and to stop prostitution.[10]

The progressive political forces in our countries suffer from that division made between the issues of women's status on the one hand, and the issues of national liberation, independence, social justice, and democracy on the other.[11]

They do not realize that the battle against dependence on foreign powers cannot be separated from that of women's dependence on men. They do not see that women cannot be liberated in a country characterized by dependency, and that a country cannot become liberated when half of its inhabitants are dependent beings, and that class exploitation cannot be ended without terminating patriarchal exploitation in the family.

Thus, they are ignoring the simplest historical truths: that the class system was founded on the slavery of women and children in the family.[12] The scholarly definition of exploitation – imposing on a person labour from which he does not obtain the wage due from producing that labour – has remained limited to work in the factory and to agricultural labour, and has not come to include women's unpaid labour in the home. Yet women's work in the home is productive labour; indeed, it is the basic labour on which all other productive labour is founded. That is, in addition to producing the labour force (producing human beings) it is the woman who, in the home, cares for the individuals who make up this labour force, nourishing them, doing their laundry, fulfilling their material and psychological needs, renewing their strength, and preparing them for the next day's work.

Despite the voluminous and heavy nature of this work, which is placed solely on women's shoulders and compensated by no wage – except food – and despite the fact that it would fit the definition of slavery and exploitation perfectly, this issue has been separated from that of the liberation of the masses.

In this way, the popular mass forces have been divided rather than united; consequently, they have been weakened in the struggle against widespread and pervasive political and economic dependency. The opposing forces have been strengthened by this division, for half of society has been distanced from the field of battle.

This half of the society has no choice but to organize itself. Thus, Arab women have begun to organize their ranks. When they do this, they do not isolate the issue of women's status from the issues of national liberation, independence, social justice, and democracy, for this standing division has not come from the Arab woman. Rather, it emerged from, and remains within and among, all the existing political forces, regardless of their various approaches.

This is the fundamental cause, in my opinion, behind the failure of progressive political movements and Arab nationalists to realize social justice and democracy. Can a man who follows dictatorial ways in his own home suddenly become democratic merely by opening the door and going out? Can he struggle against exploitation in the state when he is practising exploitation in his family?

Most political forces in our countries have remained isolated from the people. They speak at great length about the masses, but they forget that half of these masses are women. They fail to recall this simple fact except in times of crises or elections, when the votes of women are needed.

Arab women's economic weakness

No oppressed social group can become an influential political force unless the following three conditions are present:

A consciousness of the true reasons for the existing oppression and exploitation;
Political organization;
The economic ability to organize.

It must be admitted that Arab women, of all social strata, are still deprived of these three basic conditions, despite their increasing gains in the fields of education, paid employment, and participation in professional unions, labour organizations, and parliaments.

The main challenge before the Arab woman today is not to pioneer these fields, for she has already done that in most Arab countries, and has become a majority in some areas of work, such as teaching, the media, nursing, agriculture, and some industries – pharmaceutical, clothing and weaving among others.

Women represent 50% of Arab society; economic justice requires that they receive 50% of the income of the family and the state. Most women, however, and especially those engaged in production in the fields and in their homes, are living a precarious day-to-day existence on the economic margins; most are financially dependent on their husbands. Peasant women, and women working in their homes, are officially considered as 'unemployed', merely because they receive no wages.[13] The female waged labour force in Arab societies remains limited, not exceeding 12% in Egypt and probably as low as 2% in some of the Arabian Gulf nations, where Arab women are deprived of opportunities for waged labour, while foreign men obtain them.

Wage labour gives the Arab woman a measure of economic independence from the man in the family; but this economic independence has not been accompanied by social and psychological independence. A woman working for a wage shares the responsibility for family income, yet this economic partnership has not been accompanied by an equivalent sharing of authority and decision making within the family.

I have a physician friend who asked to join the Arab Women's Solidarity Association and filled out the membership application form. When the time came for payment of dues, she did not pay. We learned that it is her husband who makes decisions on such matters, even though she has an income.

A women's organization, like any other, needs financial resources as much as it needs intellectual power and cultural potential. This economic weakness – social and individual – of the Arab woman represents a great challenge faced by the Arab women's movement, if it aims to be a popular democratic movement going beyond the small urban sector that is now able to join it to reach the broad sectors of young women, housewives, students, peasant women and others who own nothing, not even the wages derived from their work.

This sort of economic obstacle faced us when we started the Arab Women's Solidarity Association and still represents a major challenge. We do not have the money to acquire accommodation for the Association's meetings. Were it not for the hospitality of the Arab Organization for Human Rights in providing a temporary meeting place, our headquarters would have been the pavement.

The organization needs means of communicating with the masses of women in the villages and cities, and with those in the various Arab countries; it needs a newspaper or magazine which can express the ideas of these women and their views on various subjects.

The organization needs to hold general meetings and conferences (like this one) in order to give our ideas greater depth and to allow for an exchange of news and the formation of links among women. All of this requires financial resources, and a modicum of economic independence with the power to make decisions concerning public activities, both social and political.

The diminishing consciousness of Arab women

There is an increasing number of Arab women working in the fields of education, culture, and the media. This numerical plenitude is not, however, reflected in the acquisition of a political or cultural strength capable of changing concepts and values hostile to women, concepts which resound through the mass media and in most existing educational and training programmes. Television, alone, is capable of weakening the consciousness of the Arab woman by showing a single advertisement which reveals a woman's body in order to sell imported goods, followed by a picture of a woman veiled to appease the conservative religious forces.

Women feel alienated in their work environments or in public activity, when they are addressed with male pronouns.[14] Alienation plays an important role in excluding them psychologically from the workplace, despite their physical presence. They suffer a division between mind and body. A woman may appear on television, for instance, but she repeats the notions which require that she be denied a role in public life or that she be hidden beneath a veil. This division is most significant in weakening the consciousness of the Arab woman and in keeping her ignorant or unaware, despite her acquisition of the highest academic degrees.

'Consciousness' and 'knowledge' still represent a serious threat to most Arab regimes and their allies among the new imperialist forces. Together, these global and domestic forces play a fundamental role in concealing existing forms of exploitation under different kinds of slogans.

It is a common and familiar occurrence in our Arab countries that laws which limit freedoms are issued in the name of democracy. People suffer from inflation and shortages of basic goods, in the name of development and prosperity. The most odious military massacres and the largest arms deals are carried out in the name of peace. The worst and most vicious pornography and crime films are shown in the name of culture and renaissance. These contradictions are suffered by men and women in our countries and in those of the Third World in general. Yet the problem of the woman is doubled, for the falsehoods go beyond her mind to reach her body.

The Islamic faith greatly emphasizes the concept of *ijtihad* – the doctrine that one must strive for knowledge and draw on one's experience in the application of the religious law. It teaches a respect for human intelligence and equality, stating clearly that there is no difference between men and women. Yet Arab regimes, grounded in despotism and exploitation, have been able, across the ages, to conceal the finest, most careful interpretations in Islam, and instead encourage the reactionary trends.

Since most of the Arab peoples suffer from illiteracy[15] and ignorance, what they know of religion is limited to the information offered by the ruling institutions through educational curricula and the mass media. As a consequence, they are daily nourished on contradictions.

The official religious establishments play their role in justifying and supporting the contradictory decisions of the rulers, by quoting religious texts. Indeed, they often give the ruler sacred attributes which virtually establish for him the status of a god or prophet, or they offer him homage and give him religiously defined justifications for instituting lifetime rules.[16]

The ascendancy of the conservative religious trends

At present, there is a growing use of the Islamic faith in Arab countries as a political weapon to brandish in the face of the opponent. All of the ruling political forces – and those outside the ruling structure – are trying to monopolize Islam, interpreting and choosing the Quranic verses, passages from the sayings of the Prophet, and words of the classical jurisprudence appropriate to their own interests.

The Arab woman continues to be the victim of this struggle. She is the weakest of the existing political elements, and does not possess a direct, unmediated, 'knowledge of religion'. Men remain the medium through which she understands religion. Naturally, men interpret the religion according to their own interests, and place themselves in the position of the powerful majority, imposing submission on women.[17]

The religious weapon has become much more dangerous with the ascendancy of the conservative religious forces as new political forces vying with each other for rule in many Arab countries, including Egypt, Sudan, Algeria, Tunisia, and Syria. This phenomenon is not limited to Arab countries, or to Islam, but is, rather, a global phenomenon which includes other religions and many countries of the world. The new imperialists – like their predecessors, the old colonialists – find in religion a weapon to divide peoples, sectarian rifts are mounted, and exploitation based on the global economic order is masked. Moreover, in the Middle East, Israel, as a racist, sectarian nation, plays its role in transforming the surrounding Arab nations into religious substates ripped apart by religious wars.

The result is that most battles taking place today in the Arab region are religiously defined, sectarian-based, resting on superficialities and reducing the multifaceted nature of Islam to a mere imposition of penalties that fall mostly upon the poor, and imposing the veil on women.

Concealed beneath the surface are international struggles over petrol and Arab wealth, Israel's occupation of Palestine, the employment of petrol revenue against the interests of the Arab peoples, spurious development projects and greater dependency, more external debt,[18] more unemployment, rising prices, and inflation.

All of this has its effect on Arab women; they are the first to be thrown out of the labour market, while voices are raised calling for their return to the home.

The links between imperialism, Zionism, and the conservative religious forces are hidden, and the economic reasons for expelling women from the wage-labour market and from public life are also concealed behind religious and moral appeals and claims.

Thus, the challenge confronting Arab women becomes immense. It is women who must reveal these facts, must demonstrate that the particular Islamic *sharia* which the conservative movements have circulated is mostly based on distorted interpretations of Islam and other philosophies that emphasize the inevitability of fate. It is women who must demonstrate that there exist philosophies and interpretations more sophisticated, just, and humane.

The Arab woman must study religion, and interpret it with her own powers of rational intelligence, rather than seeing it through the minds of others. She must link religious concepts and texts to their historical and social contexts, and develop a highly critical outlook in which rationality gets the better of tradition and imitation, and the doctrine of utility replaces a blind adherence to the literalness of the text. Certain scholars and legalists of the Islamic faith have considered that in cases where the text is in conflict with public good, the latter must take priority over the former.[19] For religions must develop and change as societies evolve.

One of the most important issues regarding which religious opinion has changed is slavery. In Islam, as in other religions, slaves – women and men – were deprived of political and civil rights. They were regarded as commodities to be bought and sold, and all that they acquired from their own labour or from gifts or donations was added to the wealth of their owner.

In classical Arabic, the word *ragiga* (female slave) is practically synonymous with the word *zawja* (wife). This suggests that the situation of wives was exactly like that of slaves.

Arab women will discover that many historical facts have been submerged since the era of slavery began. One of these facts is that women were not always slaves, or dependent on their husbands. There have been stages in human history in which women belonged to no one but themselves, indeed, women were once the goddesses of knowledge, the makers of civilizations, the creative minds in the evolution of scientific knowledge, agriculture, philosophy and medicine. These are established historical facts found in the sources of Egyptian and other ancient civilizations.

By rereading history, Arab women can learn the true reasons why they have been stripped of independence and why male authority was established over them, for these are factors arising from human society, and man-made laws, not from natural or God-given laws.

Diminishing intellectual consciousness in our nations

Just as religious consciousness in Arab countries has become falsified, so has knowledge, through an attachment to fixed texts rather than to lived experience and changing reality. The same phenomenon is duplicated in politics by attachment to fixed theories and ideologies.

Many scholars and thinkers in Arab countries continue to repeat scientific texts or concepts which have long become obsolete in modern human sciences. Among these is the concept of a fixed nature – for man or woman – or innate characteristics.[20] The phrase 'innate characteristics' confines women within the biological function of childbearing. The exploitation of the woman as a wife and a mother is overlaid by the pretext of a glorification which contradicts lived experience.

Modern human sciences have revealed that 'innate character' or 'instinctual' behaviour in fact changes and develops with social change and the development of knowledge about the environment. There is no longer something called 'innate character' which alone is influential, or carries fixed attributes, or defines a specific sort of behaviour among one differentiated group of human beings.

Veiling the mind

Just as the historical and social consciousness of women has been distorted through the falsification of history, so has their consciousness of self been warped by a spurious glorification of the past.[21] A conflict has been created between the concept of the authentic Arab personality or identity and a modern cultural consciousness based on knowledge and rational intelligence.

This is another challenge which Arab women must face: it is crucial to understand that there is no conflict between one's authentic Arab personality and modern culture. Rather, the opposite holds true: a woman's ability to grasp her history and authenticity increases as she is able more fully to comprehend modern civilization, and the new sciences, from East, West, South and North. Being female and Arab is not unlike the human personality of either sex in any other society: it is the product of that creativity which links the past with the present, the heritage with current civilization, then goes beyond both history and heritage to a future which is freer, more just and more humane.

The attributes of the Arab woman's authentic personality differs at the end of the 20th century, from that which may have characterized her at its beginning, or in the previous century, or fifteen centuries ago. Indeed, this personality changes constantly and develops to assist women's contribution to the life of the society – moving, acting, working. It is not an embroidered garment for her to wear, or a veil under which she must hide, or a fixed form into which she enters. Rather, its formation is an active movement, which demands rereading history and a reorganization and reshaping of self and society in the light of present challenges and future aims.

Heritage is a tool which all present political forces use according to their interests and their perspectives. Yet heritage loses its historical and human meaning if it does not represent all of society. In reality, half of society (that is, women) are absent and made invisible in the current struggle over the heritage and contemporary society.[22]

The Arab woman must employ heritage for the sake of greater freedom and justice for herself and her country, and as a means of change rather than as a museum for preservation of the past. This cannot be achieved without critical study of the heritage using her own intellect and analytical powers.

The freedom of Arab women is a prerequisite of a social renaissance, and a creative civilization. Freedom of thought and expression are the basic means to achieve a sound consciousness. Without this, Arab women cannot transform themselves into a political force.

The call to liberate the mind, or to raise the veil from the mind (which is the Arab Women's Solidarity Association's motto) is an essential for the liberation of the Arab person, man or woman, but especially woman. For she is ruled by two authorities (inside and outside the home) which deprive her of her rights over her own mind and body and from becoming the moving force behind her own deeds. Consequently, these two authorities efface her consciousness of herself and her position in society.

A consciousness of self is based on the acquisition of an independent personality and the attainment of a sense of authority which a woman may possess when she has not lost her sense of her own value and humanity. It is an independence embodied in deeds, not mere reactions, and in acquiring the yield of such deeds or work, material, cultural or intellectual.

A social consciousness is based on awareness of other women and a desire to unite with them to acquire the capability and power necessary in the fight to end oppression and to achieve justice and freedom for themselves – as half the society – and then for the whole society.

But women cannot achieve social consciousness without achieving a consciousness of self. Can the woman who is dependent on her husband liberate other women, or the nation, from dependency? An Arabic proverb says 'those who lack a thing cannot give it to others'. From here we derive the importance of the liberation of the self, or in other words personal liberation for Arab women, for the sake of general political and social liberation. Solidarity, and political and social organizations achieved and maintained by women help them to liberate themselves, and to gain the confidence to face their problems and overcome them.

The problem of democracy

How can Arab women become a political force? This is the pivotal question of this paper, for it is the basic challenge facing women from which the other challenges arise and flow.

In addition to Arab women's economic and cultural weakness they are scattered and isolated in their homes by virtue of their household duties. Those working outside the home are alienated within a public atmosphere which addresses them in a male-oriented language or imposes on them isolation or the veil. And those who enter the male domain of political and union organizations remain marginal.

The challenge before women is to break this isolation and to reach women everywhere, from every background and outlook. All this requires a political movement with a high degree of awareness concerning the challenges and problems facing it. Yet, in Arab countries such a movement remains fettered. Political rights in most Arab countries are severely restricted; it is difficult for any popular movement to arise without being struck down or manipulated into becoming a part of the state apparatus or dwindling down to extinction.

This problem leads to most political organizations, unions, and associations – including women's associations – becoming concentrated around the state apparatus, often becoming a mere branch of the state. They depend in their activity on the backing of the state, rather than on their own independent capabilities and popular mass strength. This is natural, as most Arab countries are ruled by a single individual or central rule which is not based on political plurality.[23]

Arab women must, therefore, understand that winning effective political power is a long process which will not show results overnight, but will require patience, struggle, and endurance.

An independent women's organization remains the sole possible means for Arab women to establish themselves among those groups which have influence in the political arena. This does not mean, however, that women should withdraw from the political establishments which already exist, such as parliaments, parties, syndicates and so on. Rather, the opposite is true. As the ability of women to participate in these political establishments grows, so does their ability to move ahead in independent organizational activity and their ability to change these establishments in such a way as to inculcate a greater awareness of the women's cause and its link to issues affecting all.

This is the basic challenge to women in all Arab countries. Despite its difficult nature, it is a challenge which can be met. The motivating forces, both conscious and subconscious, exist for the majority of Arab women. Moreover, the historical legacy exists, in the struggles of women, and in those pioneers among Arab women who possessed the consciousness and the courage to change the language that concealed their existence and addressed them as if they were men.

The Arab women's liberation movement is an extension of the struggle of those women, a free and original movement, governing itself, drawing its power from the masses of Arab women and from no other authority. It is a creative and innovating movement, deriving inspiration from pre-existing movements of Arab and Egyptian women just as it learns from modern women's liberation movements all over the world. It examines the past as much as it studies the modern branches of knowledge and the various cultures and civilizations. It believes that freedom cannot be less than whole, that human life is not divided into the public and the private, and that rights are acquired rather than bestowed.

Arab women are on the way, and there is no longer any power on earth that can pull them back.

Notes

1. This does not include Arab peasant women, who leave their homes to work in the fields and markets, without incurring protests from anyone.

2. While writing this paper, I chanced upon to read in *Al-Ahram* (12 August 1986) that the president of Tunisia, Habib Bourguiba, divorced his wife, Wasila Ben Ammar and stripped her of her title. The reason given was that she had articulated her own political views without first obtaining his permission. The same thing has happened to several Arab women who have been leaders and government ministers. As a compensation for their independent opinions, their fortune has been divorce or the appearance of a second wife.

3. This is also true of black youth movements, and other popular movements whose forces began to grow around mid-century. The women's liberation movements are among those growing popular forces fighting discrimination and distinctions made on the basis of sex and race.

4. At the end of the 20th century, multinationals and the United States have come to represent the pillars of neo-colonialism.

5. I read in the press that the Jordanian government had decided to finance the restoration of the dome of al-Aqsa Mosque in Israel. The expenses of this operation exceed $5 million. This decision is set within the framework of Jordan's new policy to aid the population of the occupied Palestinian territories in the West Bank and Gaza economically and socially. (*Al-Ahram*, Cairo, 14 August 1986, p. 1)

6. This 'mannequin' is pictured in the newspaper *al-Jumhuriyya* Cairo, 8 August 1986, p. 8.

7. Women members in Egypt's People's Assembly comprise approximately 8%. Egyptian women received the right to be nominated and elected in the 1956 Constitution; in Law no. 21 (1979), 30 seats were reserved specifically for women. In 1985, the women Assembly members were given the label 'the silent minority' by virtue of their absolute silence during the popularly-based women's struggle against the Personal Status Law that year.

In the Local Authority Law no. 43 (1979), between 10% and 20% of the seats in the Popular Councils were reserved for women. Note that the percentage of women in these councils is greater than their percentage in the People's Assembly. Moreover, the percentage of women in the Popular Councils grows as their distance from the capital and the decision-making circles increases. The percentage of women in the Minister's Council of Egypt is approximately 0.5%.

8. Among the most important rights which Egyptian women lost in the new Law no. 100 (1985) are: (a) The consideration that a husband's marriage to another woman is automatically harmful, thus permitting the first wife to demand divorce; (b) The right of a divorced woman who has custody of the children to remain in the marital home after the divorce if no suitable alternative can be found. The new law leaves the matter of finding a suitable residence after divorce and termination of the *iddat* (period prescribed by law during which a divorced or widowed woman cannot remarry) to the husband; (c) The conservative approach to the law – giving the text priority over society's best interests – is clear. This is an approach on which the Schools of Islamic jurisprudence have differing views.

9. In 1986, Iraqi women lost the right of guarantee of monogamy. (*Al-Ahram*, Cairo, 7 August 1986.) The Iraqi man was given the right to marry more than one woman. Thus, the problem of polygamy once again threatens Iraqi women. The Personal Status Law in Iraq was changed in this respect to solve one of the problems arising from the Iraq–Iran war for which women must pay, that is the increase in the numbers of widows.

10. I attended this discussion session at the Medical Association in Cairo, and some of the organizers tried to prevent me from entering the main hall where the men were sitting. I entered, in spite of them, and sent word to the chairman of the session requesting the chance for a short comment; however, he indicated through hand gestures that requests for the floor had already been closed. I left without the opportunity to speak and wrote an article commenting on the session which no newspaper – government or opposition – would publish.

11. In a seminar held in Cairo in May 1986 on the subject of 'The July Revolution', hundreds of men labelled 'Nasserists', as well as many who consider themselves socialists, Marxists, or liberals, and those from other elements of the Arab nationalist movement, were invited to attend, while, except for one woman who helped fund the session and did not attend, not one Arab woman was invited.

12. This is called 'latent slavery': slavery hidden in the family. It is a historical fact that has emerged in the works of Morgan, Marx, and Engels. Marx established that the basic profits of capitalism go back to the accumulation of surplus value derived from the labour power of women, men and children. (Karl Marx, *Capital*, Vol. I, Moscow, Lawrence Wishart, 1958, p. 737.)

Marx applied the theory of surplus value to the factory worker, but not to women's work in the household. He did not completely comprehend the issue of paternalist authority in capitalist society – just as he contradicted his own fundamental theory of surplus value and the meaning of exploitation when he neglected to place women's work in the household among types of productive labour.

13. According to the 1976 Census in Egypt, the number of women in rural areas exceeds ten million (10,170,399). Most are peasants and productive workers, yet the official statistics place them in the category of 'unemployed'.

The number of women who are housewives in Egypt exceeds ten million (10,588,377) according to the same census, and the official statistics consider them among those who have 'no profession'.

14. In a media gathering where most participants were women employed in the mass media and newspapers, the chairman addressed those present with a single phrase, 'Men of the media'. The phrase 'men of the State' or 'the men' is used to refer to both men and women. In a speech given by President Mubarak, on 2 May 1986, he repeated the expression, 'In Egypt, men are stronger than treasuries'. In *al-Ahram* newspaper, on the page of national debate, there occurs weekly the slogan 'Why is it that time deprives us of men who inform the people well and rectify the situation . . . etc.' (from al-Kawakibi). This sort of language always plays a major role in isolating women psychologically from public life, consequently causing alienation.

Fifteen centuries ago, Arab women were more aware and courageous than they are today. A delegation of women went to the Prophet Mohammed to protest about the language of the Quran and the repetition of the word 'men' without 'women', '[male] believers' without '[female] believers'. The Prophet responded to their protest and some of the Quranic verses and the hadiths began to employ the phrase [male] believers and [female] believers', 'pious [men] and pious [women]', etc. (Muhammad b. Saad, *Al-Tabaqat al-Kubra*, Cairo, Dar al-Tahrir, 1970, Pt. 8, p. 145.)

15. According to the 1976 census, 56.2% of the total populace is illiterate; among rural women, 85.9% are illiterate.

16. In Egypt in the 1940s, it was propagated that King Faruq's lineage went back to the Prophet Mohammed. In Sudan, Nimeiry was made an Imam for life. In the early 1960s, after the issuance of the nationalization decrees in Egypt, it was announced that Islam contains socialism. In the mid-1970s, after the Open Door policy was decreed and foreign capital was encouraged to enter Egypt, it was said that capitalism is inherent in Islam. At the end of the 1970s, after Sadat's visit to Israel, it was broadcast that peace agreements are part of Islam, and there was repeated the Quranic verse: 'If they tend towards peace, then tend towards it as well . . .' Earlier, in calling for war, it had been said: 'If the land of Islam is tread upon, it is the duty of every Muslim, man and woman, to wage Holy War – even women, without their husbands' permissions, and slaves, without the consent of their masters.' In this phrase, we notice the similarity between the situation of women and that of slaves in the view of some of the Islamic leadership of the late 20th century. (*Ruz al-Yusuf*, Cairo, 28 July 1986, no. 3033, p. 30.)

17. One of the most famous fundamentalist interpreters of Islam, Abu al-Ala al-Mawdudi, explains the basic concept of marriage in Islam by saying that the man is the noun or the active participle and the woman is the acted upon. The doer has the power and the acted upon is the vanquished. (In al-Mawdudi's *al-Hijab, Dar al-Turath al-Arabi lil-taba'a wa-al-nashr*, pp. 112–13.)

18. Egypt's foreign debts in 1971 amounted to $1.4 billion and jumped to $18.6 billion in 1982. The interest alone reaches 1,849 million Egyptian pounds yearly. (President Mubarak's speech of 2 May 1986.) The sum of the Arab states' foreign debts exceeds $100 billion. For the Arab oil states, the revenues from oil totalled about two thousand billion dollars between 1973 and 1982, most of it scattered between the banks of Europe and the US ($300 billion) and arms purchases ($1,000 billion) an armament which is in the service of the West.

19. Among these are the Imam al-Tufi al-Hanbali, who said: 'If the text conflicts with society's interests, the latter takes precedence over the text'. It was said to him, 'The text is better informed [possesses more knowledge] than interest, for the text came from Allah and the Prophet.' He said: 'The text is fixed, but the best interests of the society change . . . so take interests into account'; 'the prophetic text which says, "You know the matters of your world".' (Khalid Muhammad Khalid, *al-Wafd* newspaper, Cairo, 31 August 1986, p. 5.)

20. The latest thing I have read concerning this is an article by Tawfiq al-Hakim saying that motherhood is an instinct, since girls play with dolls, and that for the woman, motherhood is the most important thing in her life. The woman's role in life is to give loving care, while the man's sphere is science, religion, and comprehensive knowledge (*Al-Ahram*, Cairo, 4 August 1986). These concepts have disappeared completely from modern human sciences. It is no longer believed that boys play with pistols and girls play with dolls because of instinct or male

or female hormones, but rather because the family buys for the boy a pistol and for the girl a doll. It is training at home and at school, not male hormones, that encourages males to violence and killing with pistols.

21. I saw one American film on Egyptian women, entitled 'Veiled Revolution'. The film ends by glorifying the veiling of women, saying: 'Thus the Egyptian woman has learned her way and her authentic personality in her struggle, and she no longer imitates the western woman.' This film was shown in Egypt and many other countries around the world.

22. A number of conferences have been held on heritage and contemporaneity, in Egypt and elsewhere in the Arab region. In none of these has any research on Arab women and their heritage been presented.

23. Arab Strategy Report, issued from the Center for Political and Strategic Studies, *Al-Ahram*, Cairo, 1986, p. 322.

2. The Standpoint of Contemporary Muslim Fundamentalists*

Dr Fouad Zakaria

The issue of women occupies a position of great importance in the thinking and practice of fundamentalist Muslim groups today. This is both explicit and implicit in a host of ideas and patterns of behaviour – of both a theoretical and practical nature.

The prominent concern given to the issue of women is not due to the prestigious position of women in fundamentalist thought, nor is it the outcome of genuine preoccupation with the problems of women. On the contrary, the consistent emphasis on the position of women in the family, and their relation to men, has a twofold objective: first, to divert attention from the real problems of society and to cover up for the superficial approach fundamentalists adopt towards these problems and second, to misrepresent women's problems and to compel women to regress to their previous state of backwardness, which we thought we had broken away from many years ago.

Regarding the first objective, I would like to refer to a seminar I attended on 'Islam and Secularism' recently held at the Medical Syndicate. In drawing an example to prove the inadequacy of secular law in safeguarding our deep-rooted moral values and customs, Sheikh Yousef El Qaradawi, a prominent figure in the intelligentsia of Muslim fundamentalism, found no better example to cite than the case of the penalty for adultery. He sets up a number of hypothetical situations in which, under secular law, adulterers could escape with light penalties or even, if their lawyers were particularly competent, could be totally acquitted. The permissiveness which characterizes the attitude of secular law to the crime of adultery is, he contends, radically opposed to the values and customs of our society best enshrined in *sharia*, or Islamic law, which reserves the harshest of penalties for this crime.

This example brings to light the attitudes of contemporary fundamentalist groups to the issue of women. To select an issue of male/female sexual relationship to attest to the view that secular laws are not derived from our traditional values and moral heritage is to put exaggerated emphasis on women-related topics. While the speaker could have cited a host of other examples more relevant to women's problems and to their daily life experiences, he drew on his imagination to present us with cases of adultery

* Trans. N. El Gamal

which could pass unpunished. He assumes that the public who are suffering the hardships and grinding realities of daily life precipitated by inflation, social, political and economic crises and so on, are solely preoccupied with the worry that such an act of adultery could perchance occur and not be punished.

Further, the speaker kindles the jealousy and wrath of oriental men by citing an example in which 'honour' – a value universally prized but never precisely defined – is undermined under secular law by its failure to inflict the severest of penalties on the gravest of sins. Taking into consideration the fact that the audience on the day consisted for the most part of men, the response was evidently in favour of *sharia* law which would not be tolerant in dealing with such acts. The conclusion that logically follows, therefore, is that *sharia*, or divinely inspired law, is capable of ordering our lives better than any other code conceived by man or woman.

One single facet of women's lives – their sex lives – is given overwhelming importance. Hence, incidents related to sex feature prominently in the writings and discourses of Muslim fundamentalists. The underlying social causes leading to adultery; rooted in the conditions of life of men and women, are never explored rationally. Instead of scorning secular law on the question of adultery, a different cause and effect approach should have been adopted. The shortage in housing facilities and their exorbitant cost have led to the postponement of marriage age for the majority of young couples who – except for a limited privileged class – cannot, as their fathers did, dream of establishing separate conjugal homes. Such factors should have been considered or rather reassessed in dealing with the question of adultery: human factors cannot be ignored. Our speaker, however, looked at this problem in isolation from its social context. He selected a phenomenon capable of provoking an audience unaccustomed to think for themselves and offered them superficial, absolute views on the relations between men and women. The single example we cited above represents an entire approach which is consistently adopted by fundamentalist Muslim leaders today.

The exaggerated concern for the issue of women is but a cover to misrepresent women's real problems. A gravely reactionary view hiding behind what is loosely referred to as the 'nature of women' is propagated. The misrepresentation and distortion of women's problems is manifested in a number of dualities or paradoxical statements whose real significance remains hidden behind their apparent meaning.

The duality of emancipation and slavery

It is common for dictators to flatter their peoples and take every opportunity to heap praise on them in statements and public addresses. In their hearts, however, dictators have nothing but contempt for their peoples; their decisions are arbitrary and the more cruel their ways the softer become their words. It is a truism that the more distant a ruler from his people, the more frequently he refers to them as 'intelligent', 'wise', 'of noble descent and kind disposition'.

Some analogy may be found to the contemporary Islamic fundamentalists' attitude to women. Their teachings aim at limiting women, restricting their scope of action and ensuring their continued subordination to men. While women are accorded a secondary and marginal status, they are made to believe that this status is a great honour and distinction, and that they have attained a degree of emancipation yet unequalled.

According to fundamentalist thought, women's lives should extend into a single dimension, namely that of the family. Men, on the other hand, are conceived to lead full lives which transcend the family to extend to social, political and other fields. Restricting women's scope of action and marginalizing their role are concealed by excessive praise for the roles of mother, wife and sister: a woman is the very essence of the family, its source of love and tenderness, and so on. Neither the role of a woman, outside the family, nor the implications of this role in terms of women's economic, social and intellectual dependence on men are ever discussed. This, obviously, serves to perpetuate men's authority over women and ensure that all problems in relation to women are solved in a way that serves men's best interests.

Confining women's role to the household and leaving all other spheres of activity for men renders men the guardians of women. This fact is hypocritically wrapped up by praise for women assuming their traditional roles. Such a woman is referred to as 'the protected jewel' or 'the chaste and virtuous', for she is protected in her household, untouched by the turbulences and complexities of life. 'Protected' and 'chaste' are two adjectives derogatory to woman even if taken at face value. A woman may just be capable of protecting herself and is protected by society from certain vices and evils, but apart from this, takes no positive action in society. She is chaste because she is isolated from society and men are called upon to safeguard her chastity and keep her far removed from any contact that could 'offend her modesty' or 'risk losing her virtue'.

The expression 'the protected jewel' implies an object in one's possession, highly prized and carefully safeguarded. This flattery of women conceals an effort to objectify them as being possessed and protected. Men are not praised for 'being protected', they are expected to lead full and active lives, explore different fields and defy hardships.

The contemporary Muslim fundamentalist view of women implies a duality: overt praise and flattery and covert humiliation and degradation. Their teachings in this regard are essentially to perpetuate the degraded and marginalized state of women which is made to appear as the most emancipated and honourable.

When severely criticized for associating women as living beings with the idea of objects for protection, the advocators of fundamentalism resort – against all expectations – to an argument they believe will stifle all opposition and convince the world that their views will guarantee women unrivalled emancipation. This argument is a comparison between the status of women in pre-Islamic times and their status under Islam. I do not feel the need to quote fundamentalist writings on this topic which has been widely discussed whenever the issue of women is raised and extensively dwelt upon in writings, speeches, seminars and sermons of fundamentalists. Yet no one seems to have asked him or herself: Of what relevance is pre-Islamic practice to our lives? Is it conceivable to reduce the problems of contemporary women who lead complex lives, surrounded by problems, to a comparison that sets them in a quasi-primitive age so many centuries ago? Further, if women today are in a better position than they were many centuries ago, does this provide conclusive evidence that they have actually become emancipated?

The duality of sentiment and reason

Islamic fundamentalist literature emphasizes the sentimental quality of women. This emphasis in itself assumes a dual form: while women's sentimentality is on the one hand praiseworthy, positive and commendable, the source of love, warmth and tenderness and a cohesive force in the family, it is set against the rationality of men. To men is ascribed the ability to take decisions, to act decisively in difficult situations and to guide the family. A woman, on the other hand, 'completes' the man and adds a delicate and sensitive touch to his rationality. With such division of abilities and natural qualities between the sexes, the requirements of family life are fulfilled. Some further contend that women's excessive sentimentality, which might seem a weakness, may conceal great strength. They argue that women and men could exchange roles, as women may, through shedding tears and an appearance of weakness, come to exercise authority over men and dominate them. The main point is, however, that 'sentimentality' is seen as a positive quality that men find commendable in women.

The paradoxical natures of men and women, the duality of sentimentality versus rationality, have other implications. In facing difficult situations, women are said to be inclined to act irrationally, driven by sentiment and motivated by emotion and impulse (in the negative sense). They are incapable of making objective judgements unaffected by whims or caprices. This interpretation of women draws support from a religious heritage which judges women to be 'deficient in their intellectual abilities and religious devotion'. They are, therefore, barred from judiciary occupations, and a woman's testimony in court is regarded as equal to that of half a man.

Those advocating this view sometimes add another dimension which claims support from science. They refer to studies that produce statistical evidence to assert that women are more prone to act on impulse. From such statements fundamentalists jump to the conclusion that 'women are by nature sentimental'. Such sweeping judgements are utterly inconsistent with a scientific approach. It seems inconceivable to speak about 'a male nature' and 'a female nature' after centuries of male domination and marginalization of women's activities. Inevitably, the process of socialization over the centuries has imposed such sentimental behaviour upon women. Naturally, it is easy to confuse the outcome of social factors with 'natural' factors when it comes to conditions that have been in existence for many centuries. But common sense tells us that what is known as 'women's sentimentality' is a social phenomenon and by no means an essential part of women's nature.

We should admit that this dual view of women's sentimentality is not exclusive to contemporary Muslim fundamentalists, but predates them. It still prevails today in many trends of thought which, all alike, confuse factors resulting from women's social and economic conditions, such as their lack of independence, low legal status and persistent feeling of insecurity and inability, with the 'essential nature' of women. Muslim trends of thought, however, make use of this confusion and derive from it certain significant conclusions. Such conclusions reveal clearly the traditional duality, whereby women are praised as being the source of love and warmth in the family, but at the same time are required to remain within the confines of the home, leaving men to lead, provide, decide and dominate.

The duality of spirit and body

The duality of spirit and body may be the most important and concrete of these dualities, and is manifested in the phenomenon of the veil. The paramount importance that contemporary Muslim fundamentalists place on the veil, and their belief that it is the first and most basic criterion to determine whether a woman is on the right path of Islam, proves that concealing the body or obliterating its contours is, to them, essential in order to enter the realm of the spirit.

This matter, however, is not as simple as it may seem. It is not whether or not wearing the veil to conceal the body or to distract attention from its outlines automatically leads the woman to the attainment of a profound spirituality in both her mode of thinking and behaviour. The problem is far more complicated, and this complication renders it the most acute of the dualities.

Wearing the veil is designed to protect the body by reducing it to the level of concealed objects, undesirable and sometimes even repulsive (some modes of wearing the veil are intended to disfigure a woman). A veiled body, supposedly, attains a higher level than one that is unveiled or in a state of *sufur*. An unveiled woman vulgarly exposes her body with great skill for various purposes, not the least of which is to draw attention and admiration. But we may observe that a strong relation exists between wearing the thickest of veils and the most vulgar display of the body. They may be considered two sides of the same coin, a positive and a negative face. They both place great emphasis on the importance of the body and the insistence that it is a perennial object of desire and constant source of temptation. From this perspective, the veiled woman conceals her body to render it unattractive, and from the same perspective, the unveiled woman seeks to expose her body to render it more attractive. Despite the seeming contradiction between the standpoints of the two types of women, their behaviour asserts that for both the body is the most important thing about a woman and that man's perception of a woman's body is the basic reality in her life. Hence whereas one tries to repel such perception, the other seeks to attract it; but for both the common understanding is that men's sole purpose is to hunt women. It would be no exaggeration to say that both types of women focus only on the carnal aspect of human nature. This is further evidenced by the fact that a third type of woman exists, namely the woman who neither wears a veil nor seeks to expose her body in a vulgar manner. Such a woman is confident that her personality outweighs her physical attributes and expects others to be the same.

Wearing the veil, therefore, falls at the junction between the repudiation and denunciation of the body on the one hand, and on the other, excessive concern for the body and the danger it could pose to the woman herself as well as to others. This implicit belief in the enormous danger of the body could be exaggerated to the point that any casual physical contact, such as shaking hands, could be viewed as an ill-intentioned act and an attempt to arouse forbidden desires in the other party. Such oversensitivity to any casual touching between the sexes is the negative and protective aspect of the view which concentrates only on the carnal side of human nature.

The dual significance of the veil leads to another duality related to the behaviour expected of the veiled woman. She is supposed to have an ascetic appearance, to be suspiciously aggressive towards others and their possible motives, and to minimize mixing with men. At the same time, however, she is supposed to behave towards her husband as a wholly sexual female. While such behaviour, namely that a Muslim woman must 'respond to that which is lawful and refrain from that which is unlawful' may seem normal, the problem becomes considerably complicated from the psychological viewpoint. A woman is expected to encompass both extreme chastity and lustful sexuality. She must constantly reverse her modest, even drab appearance and prove to her husband that she is a desirable woman.[1] Can any single personality embrace such opposites and is there no risk that the contradiction between external appearance and private practice might lead to complex inconsistencies which could affect women's psychological equilibrium and harmony of personality?

The veil is supposed to produce an effect similar to that of nuns' clothing. Hence the colours of fabrics are dark, and the garments loose and shapeless, concealing body contours as well as covering the hair and at times the palms of the hands and face as well. The veil is therefore representative of a type of monasticism, but rather a partial monasticism which relates to women's external or social appearance only, whereas monasticism in other religions, such as in Christianity, involves life in its entirety, externally as well as internally. Despite the contradiction between human nature and the monastic life, we can still find harmony within it, and nuns are not subjected to a duality of an angelic, chaste outward appearance, and a private life of fleshly indulgence. It is difficult to envisage such a dual role without the corollary of a degree of personality imbalance, or a measure of hypocrisy in the exercise of one of the roles.

In addition we may point to the progressive dialectical relation between prohibition and desire. Contemporary Muslim fundamentalist practices are packed with an interlinked chain of prohibitions, including the mixing of the sexes (as a protective measure for women), the second look, the shaking of hands and revealing any part of the body whether overtly or suggestively. But prohibition has itself served to heighten desires. A young man who can neither look at a young woman nor talk to her is inclined to experience an intense sexual urge and to seek avidly for its satisfaction. The same evidently applies to young women. The more intense the urge, the stricter become the prohibitions to confront the danger. Hence, a progressive correlation exists between prohibition and desire and the resulting psychological problems are difficult to solve. Severe deprivation, like excessive permissiveness (for which we criticize Western society as though we alone were virtuous), has its own peculiar problems.

The duality of the view of man

Dealing with the duality which prevails in the Muslim fundamentalist approach to women would not be complete without revealing the corresponding duality in their view of men. The use of the veil implies that men have an insatiable appetite for women, that a man 'eyes a woman with the motives of a wolf'. Hence one of the most common justifications voiced in exhortations to wear the veil is 'to protect your bodies from the eyes of wolves'. A man is a perennial wolf, with brazen, greedy, searching eyes which fail to see women as anything but sex objects. While 'wolf' is applied to all men, the wolf always points to the other man. A husband who protects his wife from the eyes of other wolves becomes himself a wolf in the eyes of other husbands, sons, brothers, and so on. The objectification of women is once more evident in this context. Women are viewed as privately owned objects, while men strive to protect this valuable property by concealing it from the eyes of others. This property is reserved for private use, but unlike other 'desirable' acquisitions, a mere look is in itself considered a crime and a kind of violation since it implies some degree of sharing. Wearing the veil is a means of protecting women from the eyes of other wolves, and assures the 'owner' that he alone has exclusive right to 'see' and to 'enjoy'.

The image is of an ugly society in which all men are potential predators and violators of women. The only defence against universal sexual violation is for women to be totally concealed by the veil, in the same manner as wealth is kept in fortified safes which thieves cannot break into. The worst aspect of this image is that it isolates men and women from their real life problems, reducing them to two sexes each desiring and at the same time threatening the other, and overlooks the fact that they are all human beings living in a society, struggling to earn their bread, confronting economic and social problems in their everyday lives and aspiring to a better future.

The duality in the fundamentalist view of men parallels the duality in their view of women, but extends in the reverse direction. Men are accused of having an insatiable sexual appetite which can be countered only by concealing its object under the veil. Nevertheless, the Muslim fundamentalists do not urge that measures be taken against such 'wolves', but consider their condition to be irremediable, leaving them to exercise their 'wolfishness' unpunished. The onus falls on women to protect themselves by completely covering their bodies with thick fabric at all times, even throughout the intense heat of the summers of most Islamic countries.

It thus becomes clear that men, who hold the reins of society, are the originators of the game of the veil, and have, from the start, designed its rules to serve their own ends.

As an expression of extreme possessiveness regarding its 'acquisitions', even to the point of banning a mere look, oriental male jealousy sought to isolate women from all serious functions in life by according them extravagant praise for fulfilling their male-imposed role so that they would leave the more important tasks to men, and dedicate themselves to child rearing and the care and pleasure of men. The rules of the game also require that a man blames himself by blaming his own kind for being ravening wolves chasing the wives of other men. While men are not required to overcome their vices, women are required to bear their consequences in return for the verbal praise they receive.

The outcome of this situation is loss on all fronts. While men are verbally blamed and derogated, in practical terms they are straight winners. The praise addressed to women is for the purpose of helping them swallow the enormous loss to their selves as humans. The blame addressed to men, on the other hand, is intended to render the gains realized by men on all fronts seem few. The whole issue is therefore a game masterminded by men to numb women's resistance. Otherwise why would not men, at least partially, bear the responsibility of their own sexual greed and refrain rather than leaving it all for women to shoulder. But, naturally, nothing like this has ever happened, because men set the rules of the game.

I have tried to shed light on some aspects of the attitudes adopted by contemporary Muslim fundamentalists to the issues of women, and to probe into the hidden complexities underlying the declared attitudes. We have so far, however, gained only a glimpse into the dark realities about which there is silence. The field is still open for extensive research and deliberation on this highly complex topic, tightly interwoven into our social and cultural fabric.

The basic error in the Muslim fundamentalists' approach to women is that they view them as isolated from their social, historical and economic contexts, and treat them as one sex opposed to the other. They are not viewed as beings with an effective role in history, which undergoes change in a world whose primary characteristic is change. This exclusively sex-oriented view, to which women have resigned themselves at certain moments in history and under particular conditions, is taken as a constant of being in harmony with women's essential 'nature'.

I am aware that I will be severely criticized for using the terms 'contemporary Muslim fundamentalists' and 'contemporary Muslim trends'. While I admit that I have made a sweeping generalization by calling a large number of Muslim groups by a single name, despite the sharp and wide differences in perspective, I have sought to focus on their points of agreement rather than on the aspects of discord. Extremists and moderates alike are agreed on the veil and on its intellectual and psychological implications, but differ on certain inessential aspects such as, for example, its style or thickness of fabric. While contemporary Muslim fundamentalists vary widely, ranging from moderation to extremism, we should, for purposes of scientific research, seek common elements in the aggregate of variable phenomena. Had science concerned itself with particularities, dealing with them one by one, no scientific progress would have been achieved. Accordingly I have set aside differences in detail and have attempted to seek out the common elements.

Note

1. Addressing a group of veiled women in an Arab country, a Muslim fundamentalist teacher exhorted them saying, 'Be whores to your husbands'.

3. Democracy as Moral Disintegration: The Contradiction between Religious Belief and Citizenship as a Manifestation of the Ahistoricity of the Arab Identity*

Fatima El Mernissi

To highlight the basic problems of women is the first step towards the determination of the desired plan. Similarly, discovering the underlying element which constitutes the main obstacle to women's emancipation sheds light on the strategic aspects to be focused upon.

Here, I shall discuss the hypothesis that: the major obstacle which thwarts women's endeavours for emancipation is the ahistoricity of the Arab identity which views movement and change as states of social imbalance and moral disintegration. This attitude draws on its self-image as fixed, unchanging and fossilized, superior to time and change, in other words superior to the non-ending continuum of evolution. This self-identity perceives of any change, any progress as potentially eroding its character, defiling its noble descent and insulting its authenticity. When, in the 19th century, women began to voice their claims for changes in the social structure and in the distribution of authority in particular, they were considered the very incarnation of that dimension, that anathema of Arab culture, namely, the dimension of time and the awareness of self. Among the obstacles to efforts aimed at the emancipation of women, is the legitimacy of the ideology that accuses those concerned with such efforts of blasphemy and atheism.

The central theme of this chapter is time. The dimension of time which unfolds human experience is the very dimension which the Arabs today have discarded as alien to them and their identity, thereby rendering them alien to their age, confined to a fantasy world, a static world stirred by neither any development nor change: a world where the dead feed on the dreams and aspirations of the young. It may be contended that attempting to set a definition of time and to determine its relation to the Arab ethos as the main challenge to women can lead only to philosophical speculations drawing us away from reality. I would, however, like to point out that the smallest actions on the part of women, such as wearing make-up, laughing loudly or fixing their gaze on the person addressed, are all considered to be violations of the philosophy of Arab culture, let alone the call for a review of the distribution of authority and for women's participation in the decision making process. I,

---

* Trans. N. El Gamal

therefore, wish to initiate discussion on the importance of raising women's issues from the level of partial demands to that of philosophical confrontations. The main challenge women will face at the end of the 20th century is that they themselves have become a philosophical and cultural challenge to the Arab self-identity. In simple terms, we should make it clear that as Arab women calling for change, we threaten the ahistoricity of the Arab identity imposed by society under the guise of authenticity, heritage, and using the past as a reference and a model for the future.

It is proposed first to discuss the 'ahistoricity' of the Arab identity in terms of the contradiction existing between two rights, acquired at two of the most important periods of Arab history: 1) the right to religious belief, which ensured that we were able to become part of the Arab nation at the dawn of Islam in the 7th century AD; and 2) the right to citizenship, or to become a citizen of the national state established by independence from colonialism.

I shall try to highlight the contradiction between women's status as believers, on the one hand, and as citizens on the other; and to show that the very foundations of Arab society are shaken by the fact that Arab women have dared to speak out, to have an opinion of their own, to analyse and interpret events and to make certain demands. The rejection invoked not so much by the content of the demands, but rather by women's right to express their views and ask for change. The rejection is of women's right to exercise their citizenship.

I shall also attempt to reveal the source of this contradiction, namely, the absence of time from the perspective of the Arab self-identity and the inability to distinguish the actual from the non-existing or to disentangle the present from the past. The result of this situation is, in the words of al-Jabri, the Moroccan philosopher, 'the perpetuation of the old, not from within the new to sustain and authenticise it but to perpetuate it side by side with the new as a rival and a competitor.'[1]

I contend that this confusion is the cause of the weakness of the women's movement in the Arab world: the Arab personality considers itself outside the moving tide of history. In dealing with this aspect, any female Arab researcher will inevitably face the question: why does patriarchy assume the guise of legality in Arab countries, whereas in the developed countries it is acknowledged that its very structure is incompatible with the aspirations of democracy?

I believe that what is peculiar to the Arab world is not the form assumed by the patriarchal system which is similar in most societies, but rather the perpetuation of this system as an uncontestable model and an ideal, while in other societies it is open for discussion.

I would like to point out that I make no attempt to examine the status of women in terms of jurisprudence of law; I am concerned only to understand the reason for its remaining static, allegedly on grounds of legality and sanctity. In what cultural age are we supposed to be living now, in the late 20th century? This Arab cultural age will reveal itself to us in terms of the contradiction between our rights and duties as believers, and our rights and duties as citizens.

Belief, citizenship and cultural stagnation

While obedience is the decisive principle for religious belief, equality and the right to make decisions are the determinants of citizenship. In the following discussion, I will concentrate on al-Tabari's interpretation of the Quran in his famous work *Tafsir al-Tabari* to explain the quality of a female believer, and draw upon the Universal Declaration of Human Rights to delineate the essential characteristics of citizenry.

According to Article I of the Universal Declaration of Human Rights adopted on 10 December 1948 and ratified by the majority of Arab countries (Algeria, Tunisia, Egypt, Iraq, Syria, Lebanon, Libya and Morocco), 'All human beings are born free and equal in dignity and rights. They are endowed with reason and conscience . . .' This principle, which enshrines a sacred and inalienable human right, not subject to modification under any circumstance, constitutes the model for engineering relations between human beings within any institution, including the family. Where human will may conflict Article 16 of the same instrument specifies that, 'Men and women of the age of consent, without any limitation due to race, nationality or religion, have the right to marry and to found a family. They are entitled to equal rights as to marriage, during marriage and at its dissolution.' The sense of equality so strongly emphasized in this article effaces obedience.

But a female believer's relationship with her husband within the family is one of obedience. Al-Tabari's interpretation of the verse, 'Men are the protectors and maintainers of women',[2] unfolds a whole philosophy, one in which an individual exists only by virtue of their gender identity. Furthermore, the dictionary *Lisan al-Arab* defines female as 'different from male in all aspects, the plural forms of *untha* (female) are *inath* and *unuth*, assuming the same forms as *himar* and *humur*' (the plural form for donkey).

Tabari interprets verse 34 as follows:

> In saying that men are the protectors and maintainers of women, God Almighty establishes men as the guardians of their women in all that which entails discipline and restraint and for which they are duty bound to God and to their husbands. That is, because God has given more to the one than to the other. God has given more to men because they bequeath women with dowry, provide them with their needs and supply them with adequate provisions. God Almighty has therefore endowed men with superior gifts and established them as the protectors and maintainers of women; who must obey them in all affairs of their lives.[3]

Tabari cites other scholars confirming the same idea. He quotes Ibn Abbas as stating that, '. . . Men are the protectors and maintainers of women means that women must obey men in compliance with God's commandment'. To the dualistic view of obedience and support, a third element is sometimes introduced to upset this quasi-biological equilibrium. Hence Abu Zuhair on the authority of Juwaibar, quotes al-Dahik's interpretation of the verse '. . . Men are the protectors and maintainers of women' to mean that 'Men are responsible for women, they order women to obey God, and if a woman were to decline compliance, the man is entitled to beat her but not violently, since by virtue of his support and endeavours, he is her benefactor.'[4]

Tabari concludes the interpretations he cites for this verse by quoting Abu Huraira's *hadith* which he considers to be a summation of all other views. Abu Huraira states that:

> The Apostle of God, God bless him and grant him salvation, said, 'An ideal woman is one who is pleasing to your eyes, devoutly obedient to your orders and in your absence guards her virtue and your property'. Thereupon, the Apostle of God, God bless him and grant him salvation, proceeded thus: 'Men are the protectors and maintainers of women'.[5]

Obedience is, therefore, the ideal behaviour pattern that determines women's status within the family and her economic role. Obedience versus support is a duality which determines women's role as that of consumer only, while men are defined as the producers who must earn their wives' obedience.

The relationship within the Muslim family is dominated by the leadership/obedience pattern. Obedience implies surrendering the rights of freedom of thought, opinion and expression, in other words, relinquishing to others one's free will and personal independence, which are two of the most sacred of human rights enshrined in Article 19 of the Universal Declaration, which asserts that '. . . freedom of opinion and expression' is a universal right. Furthermore, Article 18 in asserting the right of all to '. . . freedom of thought, conscience and religion' provides the often overlooked link between faith and the principle of obedience.

If Muslim women were to reject their role of obedience and their dependence on and compliance with the orders of men, such behaviour would be deemed rebellious and a state of anarchy not only within the confines of the family, but extending to the realm of religion as well, since to challenge the man's authority is the same as contesting the authority of religion itself.

It is inconceivable that the role of women within the family be limited to obedience, for the principle of obedience cannot be established and take root unless the obedient party is denied the freedom to change her religion or belief. The concept of disobedience reflects this consistency advocated between obedience to the husband and obedience to God.

Disobedience: human rights as moral disintegration

Disobedience, or *nushuz*, in our Arab heritage signifies a woman's rebellion against her husband and her refusal to obey his word. Disobedience or *nushuz* as it appears in the same verse 34 of *Surat al-Nisa*: 'As to those women on whose part ye fear disloyalty and ill-conduct, admonish them (first)'* is interpreted by Tabari as follows: 'As regarding *nushuz* [disobedient women] these, in hatred and disdain for their husbands, are contemptuous of them, in rebellion, abandon their husbands' beds, disputing with them, whereas they are required to obey.'[6]

* Translator's note: In the Quranic translation used *nushuz* is given as 'disloyalty and ill-conduct' rather than disobedience.

Tabari gives a number of interpretations for *nushuz*, all of which imply disobedience to the husband or disagreeing with him. He cites both Ibn Zaid who defines *nushuz* as 'those whose disobedience ye fear', and further elaborated, '*nushuz* is disobedience and disagreement' and Ibn Abbas who said, '*nushuz* women are those who scorn their husbands' rights and disobey their orders'. Tabari himself also states that, 'linguistically, *nushuz* signifies "elevation", hence an elevated place is described as *nashaza* and *nashaz*'.[7] (Meaning that *nushuz* is to adopt a superior attitude (Trans.)).

In this context we are dealing with one of the patterns that formulate and mould human relations in a particular system. This pattern seeks to erode and destroy the will of one of the two parties. It implies that the Arab family can take decisions only after all forms of plurality have been eliminated, for plurality is synonymous with *fitna* (sedition, discord and dissent).

Fitna: the exercise of freedom of thought and expression

Fitna is commonly understood in the Arabic language to mean a plurality of views, the right to examine and analyse prevailing conditions, and to review and reconsider matters. In the *Lisan al-Arab* dictionary we find, '*Fitna* is to test or experiment with, the word was first used as follows: gold and silver are "tested" (*futinat* verb form) by melting over fire to distinguish the genuine metal from the false. *Fitan* (plural) also refers to burning, implying deceit, delusion and sin'. Thus, as defined in the Arabic language, to experiment or test, to examine the *status quo*, to reconsider and rethink a situation is sin and deceit. The rights to exercise the functions of testing, evaluation and decision making are precisely stated in the Universal Declaration of Human Rights as being the most basic and fundamental of human rights to be enjoyed by all. Since the rights of thought and expression are *nushuz*, any contribution or initiative on the part of women is interpreted as a violation of the Muslim family, a threat to the mechanics of its relationships, an erosion of its principles and a severe blow to its foundations. The charges of atheism, blasphemy and departure from orthodoxy seem to be logical consequences within a world where the principle of obedience is the focal point.

Such a world regards itself as endangered by change and movement, in which equilibrium implies stagnation. Development is the betrayal of itself, a denial of its identity which is predicated on stasis and petrification. Identity, in this cultural age is built on the illusion of authenticity, in other words, on the reproduction of a model considered to be above and beyond the dimension of time, untouched by the tide of development and change.

The pace of social change differs according to sex. Women were delegated the obedience role in the engineering of the Arab–Islamic identity; a role considered to be the cornerstone that holds together the hierarchy of power and maintains the legitimacy of the law. Thus if women demand change it is considered an aberration and a *fitna*.

What, then, is the solution? What course should we take? Raising the issue of the freedom of thought, expression and decision-making provokes a cultural crisis: a direct contradiction between Islam and human rights. This contradiction would never have occurred if the Arab identity had not purged itself of the content of time and maintained its ahistoricity.

Belief, citizenship and Arab 'ahistoricity'

Religious belief and citizenship in the Arab world are two cultural patterns which represent different and opposing theories relating to man and his will. Religious belief follows a pattern which emerged in the Arab world in the 7th Century AD, while the pattern of citizenship became known to us only in the mid 20th century. How then could we experience any contradiction between the two?

A contradiction arises and can be perceived only when two opposing elements occur simultaneously. Human beings are capable of discerning and differentiating between events, experiences and patterns inherited from former times and of assimilating this information in order to derive from it knowledge enabling them to benefit from the present and gain assurances for the future. The significance of most people's ability to arrange events according to their sequence in time, lies in the capacity to distinguish between past and present ascribing to each its relative importance. Hence a person who fails to perform the function of placing each event in its time context and confuses events which took place fifteen centuries ago with those that occurred only half a century ago is an anomaly.

It is impossible to fully comprehend the present, without an awareness of how much of the present is past experience. Had the Arab mind not been transfixed by the authority of history and instead assimilated and sifted its lessons, no conflict between the rights and duties of a believer and those of a full citizen would have arisen. Patterns of the past would never rival patterns of the present in a cultural age which kept pace with history. A mind not shackled by its history could have cherished and responded to the past, and, to some extent, benefited from it. In this respect, al-Jabri states the following:

> Arab cultural history is today in a state of stagnation . . . it does not present us with the evolution of Arab thought. It merely presents us with an antique shop or a bazaar in which cultural merchandise of former times is displayed and in which the past and the present experience contemporaneity, for the duration of the bazaar. As a result, cultural ages become mixed up in our awareness of our cultural history, and we lose our sense of history. Events of the past lose their sequence and appear simultaneous. The present becomes no more than a display of the givens of our past and, thus, in our present we live the past, with no change and no history.[8]

Independence of the Arab character from the tyranny of its history would allow it to arrange patterns according to their sequence in time, ascribe relative values to each and use them to produce a contemporary Arab culture which would employ history to construct the past and plan the future, not vice versa. While the past has its contribution, the present takes precedence. Women have a major role to play in the creation of this historical Arab culture which requires that Arab history is rewritten.

A scientific reading of history

While the Arab world devotes extensive time and effort to its history, Arab governments have not taken serious initiatives towards the establishment of suitable institutions to investigate the past in terms of the various disciplines. We are given an illusory version of the past, generated by political and ideological forces that place obstacles in the way of women, under the guise of heritage and authenticity.

What we are offered as authentic is but an arbitrary, selective and opportunistic heritage. History books provide abundant information, describing in great detail some whim of an Umayyad prince or Abbasid vizier, giving elaborate accounts of their apparel, meals, or money gifts offered to some poet or to some beautiful slave girl. While the butcher, farmer, vegetable or spice merchant might be mentioned in relation to some important personality, no insight whatsoever is provided as to their socio-economic conditions. This version of history omits any consideration of conflict between social groups and the struggle of the Arabs for centuries against despotism and for the attainment of rights and human dignity which is regarded as an unwelcome innovation. The same applies to women who strive for equality, dignity and self-realization; they too are considered strangers to the culture and to its authenticity, defiling the legacy of the forefathers and destroying the principles they instituted.

What is needed is a comprehensive, scientific reappraisal of our history. Educated Arab women have an important contribution to make, pursuing research concerning the silent groups in Arab history, the obedient party, the officially exploited sectors of society, in other words, the vast majority – among whom women feature very prominently – isolated for centuries from political decision making and from the exercise of any authority. Enriching the heritage by applying the scientific approach will bring to light the conflicts for the realization of identity and, simultaneously, revive the silent party in this heritage, namely women, who are an integral part of it.

Exploring the history of Arab women entails destroying the underlying knowledge used as a springboard to launch attacks on women. This knowledge base consists of arbitrary, selective and suppressive readings of history, a history of inequality and of despotism, a history in which Arab women who have asked for their human rights – the rights of decision making of expression and of opinion – were considered strangers to their culture and imitators of foreign women.

Emancipated Arab women in history

With the selective approach to history, each political leader can find his own examples of helpless and suppressed women whom he presents as models to be copied.

Is the history of our ancestors, therefore, a record of slavery and humiliation? Women could answer this question by a scientific reading of history. The answer will, however, continue to be in the positive as long as Arab history is limited to the annals of kings and princes, their wives and daughters from the Umayyad and Abbasid periods. As a result of the absence from history of popular groups, including women, and our failure to maintain ourselves independent of the tyranny of history, our view of the past has been distorted. Our task is to equip ourselves adequately with scientific knowledge, and to explore examples of women who have been active in experimentation and decision making, rejecting insult and vilification.

The emancipation strategy for Arab women cannot possibly generate demands (for the modification of the Personal Status Law, equal opportunities in the areas of education, work, wages, and so on) unless it emanates from a new conceptual framework. This framework necessitates woman's participation as a productive and creative force, not as an object moulded and formulated by the whims and political needs of male rhetoric.

Such a strategy can only become real if women recover all that they have lost. This includes time: its change, evolution, movement, verification and utilization in planning the future, but also, and as a matter of priority, the ability to experience the present as a fleeting moment, as a moment that could become a source of pleasure.

Freedom for the imagination: the need for a utopia
It may be observed that most statements delivered by Arab feminists have been complaints – about shortcomings, frustrations and the overwhelming sense of loss. The first step towards emancipation is to stop complaining and to add a sense of legitimacy to our aspirations. Women's dreams are presented as hallucinations; we have no right to dream, we are in fact afraid to dream, but remain immersed in our problems. Our demands for change never go beyond claims for partial reform and even these are voiced timidly.

We should respect our dreams. We should make them known to our society and to the world as legitimate frameworks for supporting the present and constructing the future. We, as Arab women, cannot regain our self-confidence unless we can release the past from the grip of the leaders. In other words, the main social and cultural challenge which Arab women are facing is to transform the Arab society from a condition in which it finds its peace and tranquillity in stagnation, to a state in which it can rejoice in moving and changing time, in the advancement of women, in unexpected dreams and unexplored paths into the future.

Notes

1. Al-Jabri, *Modern Arab Thought*, Dar al-Talia, Beirut, pp. 35–85.

2. Ali, Abdalla Y., *The Glorious Quran* (translation and commentary), Dar al-Fikr, Beirut, p. 190.

3. Al-Tabari, Abi Jafar Muhammad Ibn Jarir, Jamil al-Bayan Al-Tawil Ay at al-Quran (224–310AH), ed. M. Shaker, Dar al-Maaref, Cairo, Vol. 8, p. 290.

4. Ibid.

5. Ibid., p. 295.

6. Ibid., p. 299.

7. Ibid.

8. Al-Jabri, *Modern Arab Thought*.

4. The Influence of Contemporary Arab Thought on the Women's Movement

Iqbal Baraka

Introduction

Contemporary Arab thought – largely attributed to new ideas introduced by students returning to Egypt after studying in Europe – is considered by many scholars to have begun with Muhammad Ali's reign in the 19th century. One outstanding contribution resulting from these study expeditions was the publication, in 1834, of *Takhlis al-Ibriz Fi Takhlis Paris* by Sheikh Rifa'a al-Tahtawi (1801–73). This was the first book in Arabic to deal with the position of women, and al-Tahtawi was the first Arab thinker in modern history to advocate education for women and a change in their status.[1] By the 1870s, in *al-Murshid al-Amin*, al-Tahtawi presented what may be considered as the first comprehensive model for the emancipation of Arab women.[2]

In his two books published in the 1850s – *al-Saq alal-Saq* and *Kashf al-Mukhaba An Funun Uruba* – the Ottoman Turkish writer Ahmed Faris al-Shidiaq also wrote of the need for the emancipation of women and reiterated his views in *al-Jawaib* (his newspaper in Istanbul). Another writer, Ali Mubarak, in his book *Tariq al-Hijaa wal Tamuu alal-Bughat al-Arabia* (1871) wrote of the need for girls to receive a share in public schooling, in addition to learning sewing, embroidery and other domestic skills.

One of the more influential supporters of Arab women was al-Sheikh al-Imam Muhammad Abdin, who called for education for women and for their more favourable treatment in society. He supported Qasim Amin in his call for modification of the Personal Status Law.[3] His legal opinions (*Fatawri*) regarding the restriction of polygamy and divorce are considered to this day to be a model of enlightened Islamic jurisprudence.

In 1989, Qasim Amin's first book, *Tahrir al-Mar'a* (*The Emancipation of Women*) was published, and provoked much controversy. It is considered to be one of the three most influential books on contemporary Arab thought at the turn of the century. His contemporaries were divided into those who, many with reservations, supported his views and those who violently opposed them; in fact, opposition became so intense that the Khedive Abbas forbade Amin to enter the royal palace of Abdeen. Saad Zaghloul, Lutfi al-Sayid, Muhammad Hussein Heikal, Taha Hussein, Salama Musa, Ahmad Hassan al-Zayyat, Ahmed Shawqy and Hafe Ibrahim were among those who supported Amin's views, while his liberal ideas were denounced in 100 books and countless articles and poems. In response, in 1900, he wrote a second book, *al-Mar'a al-jadida* (*The New Woman*), drawing on examples of Islamic history and modern thought to produce a more comprehensive view of women's position.[4] The impact of his views and the influence of his teachings transcended the boundaries of Egypt and echoed in other Arab countries. Several contemporary newspapers supported Qasim Amin, including *al-Manar* (editor Rashid Rida), and *al-Jarida* (editor Ahmad Lutfi al-Sayid); articles by Malak Hifni Nassif also appeared in *al-Jarida*.

In 1925 Lutfi al-Sayid was appointed Vice-Chancellor of the newly established Egyptian University. He was asked by several of the deans to allow women with secondary school certificates to enter university. He agreed to this but cautioned against publicizing such a liberal step in the press and thus risk stirring up opposition. This was proved to be a wise precaution as when those opposed to such a progressive act became aware of it, only a decade later, they went into the attack.[5]

The issue of women's status in the Arab world has, for the last century, oscillated between two extremes of opinion: the conservative, which sees women as 'females' whose only function is to bear and rear children – plus care for the home and the husband; and the progressive, which sees them as complete human beings, equal to men, with the same rights and duties, differing only in gender. This progressive view gained an overwhelming victory through the 1952 July revolution when women won many of their rights. They not only gained equal opportunities in education, jobs, promotion, training and scholarships abroad, but pioneered areas previously restricted to men, such as the foreign service and the police. Needless to say they gained the right to the vote and to representation in parliament.

Recent statistics indicate that 15% of the labour force (approximately two million) both in the private and public sectors are women, and that this figure is increasing annually by 20,000. In 1981, there were 172 women in senior positions in the civil service (senior under-secretary of state, secretary of state and director general) as against only four in 1961.[6] In the 1983–84 academic year 2,227 women occupied the posts of professor, assistant professor and lecturer in Egyptian universities, constituting 20.5% of the senior teaching staff; over 30% of junior university teaching posts are also held by women. While these figures may be cited as official evidence of the progress of Egyptian women, the women's movement cites them as evidence of the slow progress they are making and of the obstacles they are facing. According to the 1976 census women constitute 49.1% of Egypt's population; it is, therefore, only fair to expect that their active participation in the country's workforce should reflect this figure.[7] Taking education as an indicator we find that only 34% of all university students are women; and only 33% of all graduates are women. Women with postgraduate degrees constitute only 26% of those with higher qualifications, and only 17.6% of scholarships abroad and sabbaticals are awarded to women.[8]

The 1956 Egyptian Constitution granted political rights to women. Law No.

38 of 1972, regulating the organization of the People's Assembly (amended in 1979) allocated women 30 seats in the Assembly, in addition to their right to stand for other seats, competing equally with men. Local governments Rule No. 43 for 1979 allocated 10–20% of the seats to women in addition to their right to compete for additional seats.[9] But despite all these opportunities opened for women, their political impact remains weak. The ruling party's appointment of 30 women representatives to the People's Assembly does not exactly arouse the enthusiasm of the women's movement, and the links between the two are almost non-existent. It is, in fact, quite rare for a woman representative to adopt and fight for the demands of women in the Assembly. A blatant example is the debate of 1985 over the Personal Status Law which was modified to become more humiliating to women on issues of divorce, right to the home, polygamy and so on.

Rifa'a al-Tahtawi

Takhlis al-Ibriz Takhlis Paris, published in 1834, was written during the author's stay in Paris (1826–31) and reflects his admiration for French women and for educated women in general. He realized that women possess intellectual abilities and endeavoured to enlighten his Arab readers by stating that the popular saying that a man's beauty is of his mind and a woman's is of her speech is not applicable to France; in that country what is sought for in a woman are her intellect, talents and knowledge.[10] Al-Tahtawi goes on to defend the social mixing of the sexes in France and denies that it underlies moral corruption, and points out that paying attention to appearance and dressing-up is not related to a woman's morality or virtuousness. He states that, 'The confusion on the question of a woman's virtue is not related to what she conceals or reveals of her body, for virtue is a consequence only of a good or a corrupt upbringing.'[11]

These statements may be considered as the first endorsement of the acceptability of the sexes mixing socially, and a call for lifting the veil from the faces and minds of women. The book itself may be considered the first objective study of Western society and Western women. The latter have been, and continue to be, the object of some Arab men's fertile and sick imagination. Hence al-Tahtawi's admiration and respect for French women must have come as a novel discovery, an exploration into hitherto unknown worlds. He presented it as another concept in the same way that he introduced journalism, magazines, the parliamentary system, theatre, opera, the circus, and so on to his contemporaries for them to choose what suited them to adopt and replicate.

Muhammad Amara, the Islamic scholar, says of al-Tahtawi

> he was not a mere translator of Western thought and civilisation into the Arabic language, he was a contender, out to raise the consciousness of his people and his nation . . . in fact the whole of the Eastern and Muslim worlds. His writings and descriptions on politics, the constitution and . . . bourgeois democracy were meant to open the new horizons of

democracy for his countrymen to explore. It was a call for the East to overcome the odious and tyrannical marshes of individual rules.[12]

Women's liberation is an integral part of an individual's civil liberation and thus, in the minds of thinkers and writers, was always connected with political freedom. In *al-Murshid al-Amin Fi Tarbiat al-Banat wal-Bainu*, (*A True Guide to the Upbringing of Boys and Girls*) al-Tahtawi's second book, the author expresses his astonishment at the respect accorded to women in France: no veils, no beatings, no insults, no limitations. Women are considered to add grace to society, are free to choose their spouses, to travel, and to express their feelings in books that are widely circulated and quoted. This book, which was translated into Turkish, had a far-reaching impact on Arab society, then much influenced by the rigid conservatism of the Ottoman Empire. On the equality of the sexes Tahtawi stated that 'Women are equal to men. They each have a human body, the same needs and the same external and internal senses. The two sexes are almost identical in every aspect except for minor differences in femininity and masculinity and their necessary sequlae . . .' He did not consider 'femininity' a weakness and explains the physical frailty of some women as a product of environmental and social conditioning in upbringing that is possible to reverse, citing Greek women as an example. He asserted that women's perceptiveness and intelligence compensate for their physical weakness, and rejected charges that they are sly and malicious. That the role of women is that of 'vessels of procreation' is refuted, as, with profound evidence to the contrary, is the alleged *Ahadith* (Prophet Muhammad's sayings) prohibiting education of girls. He uses his arguments to substantiate his call for women's education not only in basic literacy but in the arts and sciences, and sees the link between women's education and work, 'if the need should arise, a woman could do a man's job, within the limits of her abilities'.[14]

His insight into the effects of work on women's character is unequalled by many of our contemporaries. He contends that:

this [work] will occupy women and save them from laziness. With idle hands their mouths will be filled with lies and gossip and their hearts with deceit and caprice. Work protects a woman from improper behaviour and draws her closer to virtue. If idleness is hateful in men, it is even more reprehensible in women.[15]

Al-Tahtawi encourages the mixing of the sexes at the workplace, drawing on the example of the prophet Shnaib cited in the Quran: Shnaib sent his young daughter to call young Moses and the encounter ended in marriage. Al-Tahtawi goes further to endorse the legitimacy of girls falling in love. He appeals to parents to consider the sentimental attachment of their daughters when deciding on their marriage: 'the greatest favour done to a girl is to marry her to the one she loves and has chosen herself'.[16] He calls for friendship between married couples for 'friendship ensures perfect harmony, unity and love between the man and his family in all their doings'.[17] For al-Tahtawi, respect is 'the only means to perpetuate love between the spouses'.[18] For him there is a direct relationship between the type of love that prevails in a society, the nature of this society and the type of government ruling and its administration of justice; he classifies them as barbaric and ignorant or civilized and cultured.

The issue of love and respect between the spouses seems to dominate the writings of al-Tahtawi to such an extent that Amara places him on an equal level with Ibn Hazm (994–1064) the author of *Tawq al-Hamam fil-Ulf wal-Ilaf*. Ibn Hazm, however, deals with love as a science whereas al-Tahtawi speaks of love as an art emanating from the finest sentiments, from knowledge and the arts.

Al-Tahtawi was the first writer to draw the attention of Muslims to the ideas of the French revolution (liberty, equality and fraternity), the first to apply these concepts to the status of women and to exercise them in his personal life. The document of his marriage to his cousin testifies how he practised his beliefs; he denied himself the right to polygamy, to divorce and to the holding of slaves. Slavery, which was an acceptable institution at the time, was abominable to him. He freed both his male and female slaves but continued to look after their well-being, providing for their needs and even bequeathing them some of his land for their support.[19]

Taklis al-Ibriz's influence on contemporary society

Muhammad Ali (then ruler of Egypt) was fascinated by the ideas in this book and ordered it to be circulated in his court, government offices, and schools. It was twice reprinted (1834 and 1849) during the author's lifetime, and a third time (1905) after his death; it was also translated into Turkish. Al-Tahtawi continued his activities in teaching, translations and management, thus successfully spreading his ideas, for 40 years after the first publication of his book.

Qasim Amin

Qasim Amin is considered to be the first true 'Emancipator of Women' as the majority of his works was exclusively devoted to women's issues. His two books *Tahrir al-Mar'a (Women's Liberation)* (1899), and *al-Mar'a al-Jadida (The New Woman)* (1900) provoked heated debates amongst his contemporaries. He is considered by some, however, as the first Egyptian secular thinker and not only the 'woman emancipator', as the idea of freedom was foremost in his thinking. He advocated freedom of the mind, freedom of the conscience and freedom of the feelings. His interest in women emanated from the main focus of his interest: freedom in general. *Tahrir al-Mar'a* marked the end of an era at the turn of the century, while *al-Mar'a al-Jadida* heralded the new century and a new era; the influence of these two books was deep and far reaching. Conservative writers to this day find them a source of provocation to be analysed and refuted. They see Qasim Amin's ideas as dangerous because Amin was not simply a layman but a respected supreme court judge. He received his degree in law in 1881 and was a prize-winner; in 1885 he went to Montpelier on a scholarship to further his studies. While in France he met Jamal al-Din al-Afghani and al-Sheikh Muhammad Abdin (two well-known contemporary thinkers) and became the personal interpreter for the latter. On his return to Egypt he served in several judicial posts in smaller towns until at the age of 31 he was assigned to his post in the supreme court.

Among his other activities was a campaign with Saad Zaghloul, the nationalist Egyptian leader at the time of British–Turkish rule, to establish the national Egyptian University; a regular column in the newspaper *al-Mu'ayad*; and his attendance at Princess Nazli Fadil's, where all the prominent men of politics and literature regularly met.

The rare depth of knowledge, insight and comprehensiveness of Qasim Amin's two books had an immense impact on the public. He seemed to have mastered both Eastern and Western cultures and took a very firm stance on the reactionary *Salafi* trend and the inflexible thinking of the day. He was the first to openly attack the custom of veiling. He did not call for its total abolition, but staged its removal by strictly adhering to the statutory veil as a first step towards its elimination. He violently attacked polygamy and called for its limitation and also criticized the man's absolute power in divorce and called for arbitration by impartial bodies – as the Islamic Shari'a advocates – leaving the final judgement to the courts in divorce cases. It is amazing that these last three issues remain unresolved and continue to arouse major controversy amongst writers and thinkers to this day.

Qasim Amin also saw a close link between politics and the family in every society. He stated that: 'Wherever men have undermined women and treated them as slaves, they have undermined themselves and lost their own sense of freedom, while in countries where women enjoy their personal freedom, men enjoy political freedom.'[21] He considered work a necessary prerequisite for women's liberation:

> Denying women their first duty, namely from becoming qualified to earn their own living, has led to the loss of their rights. Men, having assumed responsibility for all matters, have equally assumed exclusive rights for themselves. Women are then left with the fortune of a pet whose owners graciously provide essential needs in return for some playful times.[22]

The ideas in Qasim Amin's books were of paramount importance. He called for equality in primary school education for boys and girls; for all the jobs in the civil service to be open to women; and contended that Egyptian women were capable, and that to bar them from work was a loss to the nation: '. . . since women constitute half of the population of any country, keeping them shackled by ignorance can only deprive the nation of half its potential . . .'[23]

More than 85 years ago, Qasim Amin's ideas had an enormous impact on his society. Some of his contemporary enemies had called for his execution, his house was attacked several times, and newspapers and magazines carried articles and poems responding to his ideas. Books were written to evaluate his thoughts, the most prominent of which was that by the economist Talaat Haib.

The birth of the women's movement in Egypt may be dated to the publication of Qasim Amin's books. One of those deeply influenced by his writings was *Balithat al-Badya* (The [She] Searcher in the Desert), Malak Hifny Nassif (1886–1918) the first woman orator. She had just turned 20 when Qasim Amin died, in 1908. When Qasim Amin first published his two books and started the controversy over women's issues she was 14. It was only logical that she should push women's demands beyond his frontiers, but living in such a constrained society she had to be more cautious. This explains why she sometimes opposed *sufur* (state of uncovering the face) not out of belief in veiling but because she thought the time was not ripe for such a revolutionary act. She advocated introducing change by gradual stages and believed that women should first be educated; and young men disciplined. The third most important argument for caution was that Eastern culture should not be assimilated into Western culture for fear that Egyptians would lose their identity and hence their enthusiasm for independence.

Despite her middle-of-the-road stance on the questions of *sufur*, Malak Hifny Nassif was a strong advocate of a woman's right to choose whether or not to wear a veil. To her it was not a man's decision. She stated that:

I admire men's concern for our affairs and the affairs of their nations. However, we never claim to feel for them nor assume what they want. How, then, can they decide for us with the confidence of those feeling the malady and knowing its cure?[24]

She goes on to assert, 'A serious unveiled woman is far better than a flirtatious, licentious woman wrapped in the thickest silk and covered by the heaviest veil.'[25] In answer to those who accused her of double standards, she wrote a poem, arguing that the veil is one form of negative resistance and a woman's weapon against men's immodesty. She saw the veil as a condemnation of men's moral standards rather than as a submission to their will and argued that the day women decide to remove the veil out of their own free will is the day when they have more trust in men and respect for male moral standards. This day, she thought, would come when women were equipped with education and virtue against men's immorality.

M. H. Nassif defended women's right to work and answered all the arguments claiming that it constituted competition with a man's main function in life. Her counter-argument was that historically, spinning, weaving, serving, baking, and so on, were all women's work and that peasant women still do this work.[26] She rejected men's patronizing attitudes and asserted the principle of personal freedom for women to decide whether to stay at home or go out to work.[27] Furthermore, she promoted the right of young women to choose their line of study and not be restricted by the views that only certain subjects are suitable for girls, believing that such restrictions are '. . . frustrating and a setback'.

She also attacked the view that a woman's place was in the home. Here we can see the clear influence of Qasim Amin when she says:

> having completed my domestic work I felt bored and lazy. Why shouldn't I take my share of fresh air by going to a suburb where God created nature for all his creatures and did not keep it in boxes labelled for men only?[28]

M. H. Nassif discussed her ideas at women's gatherings in public places, but she found it necessary to maintain reserve in some of her ideas. Compared to Qasim Amin there is all the difference between a free thinker addressing an enlightened élite, and a teacher at a girl's school who must be careful not to shock or offend the young girls in her care. She had to help the women at these public gatherings to grow in virtue in the conventional ways and not provoke the conservative elements in society against them. She did, however, go further than Qasim Amin by calling for compulsory primary and secondary school education for girls of all social classes.

The image of women in the cinema and novels

There are other examples of contemporary Egyptian writers who contributed to the cause of women and played a positive role in pushing women towards education, work and an active role in many fields, among others, Ahmed Lutfi al-Sayid, Salama Musa and Taha Hussein. But opposed to them were those who had a negative effect on the women's movement by undermining their efforts, by ridicule and calling for their confinement to the home. Sadly this trend was predominant in the cinema and in fiction writing. The number of Egyptian films that depict women in despicable and subordinate roles by far exceeds those that reflect a true image of women's lives; women's movements have organized several seminars in the last decade to seek the reasons for this. Possibly the Egyptian cinema has been influenced by the image of women in the romantic Egyptian novels.

In 1905, Muhammad al-Munalhi published his novel *Hadith Issa Ibn Hisham*. Although a contemporary of Qasim Amin and witness to many of the debates on Amin's two books, he ignored women completely and restricted his novel to a world of men only.

Zeinab, a novel by M. Hussein Heikal (1914) was published under the superscription of 'Written by an Egyptian peasant', and subtitled 'Rural Scenes and Morals'. Made into the first Egyptian feature film it sets the theme for what later became the pattern for depicting women's images in Egyptian literature, that is reducing her to a mere symbol. *Zeinab* does not truly exemplify the Egyptian peasant woman. At the turn of the century, World War I, Egypt was in the turmoil of nationalistic feelings against British colonial rule; Mustafa Kamil's speeches filled the horizons and Muhammad Farid captured people's imagination with his sacrifices. Zeinab – the central character – is oblivious to all this and suffers no social or economic injustice. Her encounter with the landlord, at whose house she works, is a scene of affection and sympathy. She embraces his son Hamid and exchanges kisses, though they are not in love. At her in-laws' house she embraces her lover, Ibrahim, and exchanges passionate kisses with him, even though she is married to another man. When her lover is conscripted for military service, she regrets that she did not give herself to him 'as a memory to cherish and give her comfort'. Would the reader in 1914 sympathize with such an image of woman and her deep hidden feelings or would it not rather confirm their belief that women are untrustworthy and are naturally inclined to vice?

This image of women is repeated in two novels by Ibrahim al-Mazni: *Ibrahim al-Katib* (1931) and *Ibrahim al-Thani* (1943). He ridicules all his female characters and has them fall in love with him 'at first sight', then give in totally to his desires in endless embraces and kisses. They have a sexual relationship and when one becomes pregnant she refuses his offer of marriage as she disapproves of marriage ties.[29]

The only novel written by al-Aqad, *Sarah* (1938), presents the same sick, distorted picture to undermine and limit women and to promote suspicion of their integrity. Sarah is 'a bundle of nerves' whose sole preoccupation is to inflame her lover's jealousy, to attract his constant attention. The novel attempts to answer the questions in Humam's (the hero's) mind: Did Sarah betray him? With whom? And why? But it never succeeds in finding the answer. We are left with the belief that women were created to torture men and that by nature they incline to vice rather than to virtue. One critic commented on the novel:

> Since Sarah symbolizes the instinct in such an absolute manner, we should not expect the author to establish any association between her and her social environment. The environment can have no influence on persons born into the feminine sex. Females are born females, live as females and die as females, unaffected by social environment, upbringing or any other circumstance. Sarah does not experience tension, worries or pain, despite her life being torn in all directions. Still all her actions arise from this instinct that completely dominates her. We do not sympathise with her crises and are not expected to allow her more than our understanding.[30]

None of the literary writings of the first half of the 20th century contains any female character that truly reflects the hopes, aspirations or sorrows of women. They are all women passionately in love seeking emotional adventures and ever moving in men's orbits. This is true of the novels of Abdel Hakim Abdalla, A. Gouda al-Sahhar, Yousif al-Siba'i, Ihsan Abdel Quddus and Tewfiq al-Hakim. All are hostile towards independent, educated ambitious women whom they see as their enemy. A critic commented that:

> their female characters are unconvincing, unjustifiable, evoking indignation rather than pity. Even when they depict women as students or workers, the images presented are socially and intellectually underdeveloped. This emanates from a unilateral biased view which engenders the negative attitude that thwarts both reality and the art.[31]

These observations apply to the characters of Leila in the novel *Laqita* by Abdel Hakim Abdalla; two of al-Sahhar's heroines, Zeinab of *Shagarat al-Liblas* and Kawthan of *Qafelat al-Zaman*; and to Huda of *al-Niqab*. Huda is a veiled young lady, so Hussain, the hero, chooses her for a wife thus abandoning Alya, his rich emancipated cousin who loves him. After the birth of their first son, however, he discovers that his veiled wife is in love with Jamal, his best friend. Thus the reader is left with the impression that neither the veiled, nor the unveiled emancipated woman is right for the author. This impression is constantly created by many writers and is particularly true of Ihsan Abdel Quddus's novel *Ana Hurra* (1953) (*I am free*), thought to be a very emancipated novel for its time which could corrupt young women. (We were able to read it only under the covers.) In this novel the slandering of women reaches its climax. Sex is represented as the woman's ultimate goal when she is seeking independence. Amina, the main female character, is young, has money, good looks, a good family heritage, education and work. She proudly repeats slogans about political rights for women until she meets Abbas, a young rebellious lawyer, and is stupified by her love for him. They live together, unmarried, for eight years with no sign of her participation in any of his political work. But the novel overflows with elaborate descriptions of love scenes and Amina's ecstacy. No struggle, no aspiration, just a vacuum with sex as the ultimate goal for Amina, and for that matter all women calling for emancipation.

Not surprisingly one critic saw that:

> sex in the novel *Ana Hurra* embodied the real crisis of women's emancipation. If the author had meant to present sex as the essence of the human experience as it was lived by Amina, his reporting journalistic style has imprisoned him. It is a style that describes the external events without probing deeply into the characters. By stripping the novel of its artistic wrappings and dissolving the fine but necessary web of connections that bind the events to the character he has defeated his purpose.[32]

It is unfortunate that most of these novels have been dramatized for radio, television and the cinema thus propagating these ideas amongst simple, illiterate or quasi-literate people. Hence the germ of bias and mistrust of women has spread from the limited circles of novel readers to infect the population at large.

Conclusion

Thus contemporary writings on women can be broadly divided into a stream of scientific egalitarian thought which sees the cause of women as inseparable from the freedom of the Egyptian people, and a literary stream that can see women only as an object or a symbol, an abstract idea. This second group cannot shake off their childish and immature thoughts when dealing with women. Of course, many writers never dealt with women while others fluctuated between support and condemnation.

Two decades into the July (1952) revolution, the whole concept of women as a separate group was thought to be a divisive and reactionary form of thinking. Many refused to consider it a separate issue in its own right, but one to be tackled only within the broader reform of society. The 1970s arrived with the age of 'Science and Faith' and Arab women found themselves in a trap. In Egypt, reactionary writers surged forward and overwhelmed the intellectual circles. Voices called loudly for women's return to the home as the sole remedy for many perceived calamities in society, a call that spread quickly amongst the girls and young women in schools and in the universities. Long rejected ideas were reintroduced and propagated under the name of religion and the revival of Islamic heritage. The ideal society was seen to be that of early Islam. Books by ancient Islamic writers, who had lived hundreds of years ago, were tirelessly searched for guidance on current affairs. Women were attacked by their proponents and adversaries alike. The reactionary right accused them of deserting their religious values and their cultural traditions, charging them with imitating Western women and following the illusion of modernization. The progressives, on the other hand, accused them of weakness and of allowing themselves to be defeated for not taking up the opportunity offered to them by the 1952 revolution and the socialist reforms of the 1960s.

The Egyptian woman suddenly found herself at a crossroad, unable, single-handed, to confront the problems of the economic crisis created by the 'open door policies' of the 1970s, the receding influence of positive Eastern values, the breakdown of social and family ties, and the blind imitations of the worst aspects of Western culture; while the reactionary fundamentalist voices ever more loudly denounced these and directed their wrath at women, propagating the belief that women's return to the home, away from public life would cure all these social ills.

In the final count it is up to women themselves to decide what to do next. They may choose to submit and retreat to the position of their grandmothers centuries before or they may choose to resist, join ranks and fight back, thus creating a true presence for themselves in the political arena. It is through this active presence in politics that women will be able to correct the balance in other fields and promote their true image in arts and the literature. They can then re-evaluate and discuss the ideas of past and contemporary thinkers, refute what is obsolete and receive what is positive.

For centuries the Arab woman has been the receiver of ideas rather than their creator, has implemented other people's decisions, and submissively followed rather than led or pioneered. Now, after 50 years of education and mass involvement in work in many fields, it is high time she became a decision-maker alongside men.

Notes

1. Amara, Muhammad, *Qasim Amin: The Complete Works*, Arab Corporation for Research and Publications, p. 13.
2. Ibid.
3. Wadi, Taha, *Women's Image in the Contemporary Novel*, Dar al-Maare, p. 34.
4. Ibid., p. 37.
5. Fouad, Neimat A, *Literary Giants*, Aalam al-Kitab, p. 35.
6. Ministry of Information Publications, 'The Egyptian Woman', 1985.
7. Ibid.
8. Ibid.
9. Ibid.
10. Tahtawi Rifa'a R. *Takhlis al-Ibriz Fi Takhlis Paris'*.
11. Ibid.
12. Amara, Muhammad, *The Complete Works of Rofaà Rafi al-Tahtawi*.
13. Tahtawi, R. R., *Al-Murshid al-Amin Fi Tarbiat al-Banat wa al-Bainu*.
14. Ibid.
15. Ibid.
16. Ibid.
17. Ibid.
18. Amara, Muhammad, *A Study on R. R. Tahtawi*.
19. Quorani, Izzat, *Contemporary World Thought*, Said Raafat Publishing Press, p. 185.
20. Ibid.
21. Amin, Qasim, *Al-Mar'a al-Jadida*.
22. Amin, Qasim, *Tahrir al-Mar'a*.
23. Ibid.
24. Nassif, Majd El Din Hifni, ed. *The Collected Works of Bahithat al-Badya*, Heritage Series Ministry of Culture & Information, p. 275.
25. Ibid., p. 273.
26. Ibid., p. 74.
27. Ibid., p. 75.
28. Ibid., p. 84.
29. Al-Katib, Ibrahim, Dar al-Shaab, Cairo 1970, p. 205.
30. Badr, Abdel Mohssin Taha, *Development of the Contemporary Arab Novel*, Dar al-Maaref, Literary Studies Library 32, p. 273.
31. Ibid.
32. Shukri, Ghali, *The Problems of Sex in the Contemporary Arab Novel*, Egyptian Public Corporation for Writing and Publications, Cairo 1971, pp. 192–3.

5. Palestinian Women's Movement in the Israeli-Occupied West Bank and Gaza Strip

Rita Giacaman and Muna Odeh

In the recent past, considerable attention and enthusiasm have accompanied attempts to study the lives and concerns of Palestinian women.[1] These efforts cannot but be commended; in general, they have succeeded in bringing Palestinian women into the limelight as actors and not just as victims. Nevertheless, they remain problematic in that they fail to place the question of women in a proper context. In the context of Israeli military rule in particular, a balance between the national political problem and the other conflicts that govern the lives of women is the essential key to a coherent and comprehensive analysis of women's position in Palestinian society.

This chapter attempts to redress this balance. It is not intended as the last word about women under occupation, but as an introduction to a debate by, for, and about Palestinian women. It attempts to extend the current debate among those of us who live under Israeli military rule beyond the boundaries of the West Bank and Gaza Strip. It is primarily governed by a drive to compare our experience with that of others and by a desire to look outside the Palestinian context for solutions to what seem questions impossible to answer. It deliberately omits a discussion of the woes that befell Palestinian women as a result of military rule, and concentrates on dealing with internal problems in the nature of Palestinian society.

At issue here is the way in which women's liberation is conceived under conditions requiring national liberation. What seems to be an impossible knot is the primacy of the national political conflict, under which all other conflicts in the lives of women are either reduced to secondary positions, or disregarded. It is a question of serious dissociation between theory and practice. While the formal debate – depending on which women's group we are discussing – might theoretically admit to the existence of other than national political contradictions as factors governing the lives of women, that acknowledgement is usually firmly shelved.

This imbalance in the Palestinian women's liberation formula has a long history; it dates back to the early 1920s, to the emergence of an organized Palestinian women's movement[2] (an informal women's network has existed over the centuries, of course). Under the leadership of such women as Hind al-Husseini and Zlikha al-Shihabi, the Palestinian women's movement was born. For the first time, Palestinian women moved from the domestic sphere to that of public life, joining their husbands, brothers, and sons in protesting against the Balfour Declaration and the Jewish migration to British Mandate Palestine. They participated in a variety of activities: joining demonstrations, sending telegrams of protest and even setting up first aid stations to attend to the needs of guerrilla fighters. At a later stage and especially during the late 1940s and as the Palestinian catastrophe (in the Palestinian political lexicon this is the creation of the state of Israel, with the resulting dispossession and dispersion of thousands of Palestinians) was taking shape, women's organization in the part of Western Palestine that did not fall under Israel extended their efforts beyond their traditional concern for the poor in their communities. They did everything possible to absorb the shock and care for the refugees that flooded the West Bank and Gaza.

These organizations were especially active in the 1947–50 period, between the time when the British Mandate authorities 'deserted the population' as some of the contemporary women's movement leaders put it, and the time Jordan annexed the West Bank and created its state, and the United Nations Relief and Work Agency was established to care for the refugees. During this period, the women performed the crucial function of substituting for state services. They set up training centres for women nurses, establishing the profession as socially acceptable and respectable for women; they successfully operated first aid stations where even minor surgery was performed; they campaigned increasingly for donations, ranging from canned foods to clothes to money; they organized soup kitchens and succeeded in getting even very bourgeois society women to participate in cooking; and they washed and mended the clothes they had collected and distributed them to those who needed them.[3]

It appears almost certain that the birth of formal Palestinian women's organizations as well as the establishment of women's role within society (as opposed to their previous seclusion within the domestic sphere) occurred simultaneously with Palestinian attempts to fend off the injuries resulting from aggression and dispossession. The Palestine question provided the motive and platform propelling women into a new arena as visible actors. But it also served as a major deterrent to the movement's further development at a later stage.

While the activities of that generation of Palestinian women were remarkable and laid the foundation for women's legitimate participation in social, political, and economic life, they were nevertheless straitjacketed by the conceptual formula that equated colonialism and/or occupation with the debasement of women's status. This formulation, which assumes that Palestinian society is homogeneous and does not take into consideration class and gender relations and conflicts, was upheld by the (male) leadership, since, conveniently, it did not threaten the *status quo*. The leaders of the women's movement in the first part of the century had been primarily sisters, wives, and daughters of the political leadership which represented the interests of the élite and landed families in Palestine.[4] Although major reshuffling took place in the 1950s and the 1960s, culminating in the creation of the Palestine Liberation Organization and the takeover of its leadership by the middle class, those activities did not radically affect the activities and aspirations of the women's movement. While one might argue that the conceptual formula took many forms over the years, its content nevertheless remained the same. For over 50 years women's activities remained confined within a formula devoid of the concept of internal social contradictions independent of colonialism or occupation, and without an analysis of the relation of those contradictions to the oppression of certain sectors in Palestinian society, especially women.

Such a unidimensional view of women's lives necessarily had a dramatic impact on the structure, vision, and activities of women's organizations in the Occupied Territories. Until the birth of the new movement in the late 1970s, both the structure and the function of women's organizations in the West Bank and the Gaza Strip mirrored the middle-class nature of these organizations. Initially, most took the form of charitable organizations, with highly centralized structures, located almost invariably in towns and urban centres, with middle-class, town-dwelling women overseeing the work, understood as a philanthropic expression of middle-class values. Charity was the guiding principle at the heart of their interest in society and their activities in women's organizations. Well-respected middle-class women participated in 'helping the poor'; most of the poor that they saw were women, partly because they were women and partly because women were the poorest sector in Palestinian society. This ideology of charity was so pervasive as to reflect itself even in the names some societies chose for their organization: *Asdika' al-Marid* (The Friends of the Sick), *Dar al-Yatim* (The Home of the Orphan), *Jam'iat Bisat al-Rahmah lil-Nissa' al-Orthodoxiat* (the Carpet of the Forgiver's Greek Orthodox Women's Society) and *Jam'iat Hamilat-al-Tib li-Ighathat al-Ba'is al-Marid* (The Carriers of Goodness Society for the Relief of the Miserable Sick). Activities were conducted 'from above'. Middle-class women defined the needs of, delivered services to and, indeed, were charitable towards village, refugee camp, and poor women.

There were exceptions, especially among such women's societies as *Jam'iat 'In'ash al-'Usra* (The Family Rehabilitation Society) in al-Bireh and others that proliferated, intensifying their activities especially to provide basic services under Israeli military rule. Their work had a definite political content which later became known as *al-Sumud* (*al-Sumud* or 'steadfastness' in the Palestinian context has come to mean the attempt of Palestinians to stick to the land, despite all the pressures that force them to do otherwise). But they, too, remained essentially a middle-class movement: women were being trained in jobs that serve as back-up for men's work; to be good housekeepers and mothers; and to have as many children as possible because this is their *wajib watani* (or national duty). The women's lives were not considered important. Thus while the more nationalistically inclined societies did and still do contribute considerably to the delivery of basic services to the poor, and especially to women, their activities fall short of being totally in the interest of women.[5]

Nevertheless, the role of the earlier women's movement should not be underestimated. Despite all the criticisms one might have of this movement in retrospect, given the context within which it evolved it was revolutionary. The women of the older movement fought to legitimize a social role for women and, therefore, set the stage for the development of a more radical movement.

A breakthrough did take place in the late 1970s. Several factors led to the crystallization of a radically different women's movement. They included a further development of Palestinian society; the reality of occupation; the emergence of a small but nevertheless important sector of educated women; and perhaps the more important factor of the birth and development of new forms of women's organizations. From centralized charitable societies dominated by middle-class women and their views, busily involved in distributing charity, to peasant, refugee and poor, town-dwelling women, the progressive movement of the women's committees developed.

In contrast to the 'older' movement, the progressive committees' movement was founded on the attempt to mobilize rural and refugee camp women. The mood of the time was dominated by Palestinians' sense of failure to politically mobilize in the Israeli-occupied areas.[6] Activist women were beginning seriously to consider the need to mobilize this important and neglected sector of Palestinian society, and to bring it into the ranks opposing Israeli military occupation. The move to penetrate the villages took the form of informal women's committees that sprang up in hitherto unknown or inaccessible areas. This move radically dislocated the system, as it involved the sudden visibility of women previously invisible to society. The women's movement's confrontation with miserable living conditions, high illiteracy rate, bad health conditions, absence of such basic services as nursery schools and drinkable water, and so on, necessitated its inclusion of gender relations into the women's liberation formula. This shocking experience made it evident that it was impossible to begin to consider politically mobilizing underprivileged women before fulfilling their basic needs. One could not expect such women to keep up with Palestinian politics (which have been known to defy the expertise of the most knowledgeable university professors) when they could not even read or write; and when tradition and protocol prevented them from even moving about freely or having the leisure to read and study.[7]

Such an unexpected and unacceptable predicament came as a shock to many of us. We had often thought, or had liked to think, that Palestinian women were different from their Arab sisters. According to the logic, the high level of education and the advanced stage of development of Palestinian politics and society relative to other Arab countries should have created a context that had advanced the position of women to equal that of men. But the realities of life in villages and refugee camps imposed a new understanding and, therefore, new possibilities for analysis. We found grave disparities in Palestinian society: between town, country, and refugee camp; between different groups within villages and refugee camps; between the rich and the poor; and between men and women. Thus, the rediscovery of the village and refugee camp led to the emergence of a new type of struggle, one that attempted to change the predicament of these neglected women, to help them solve their daily problems so that they could then develop their own roles and positions in the popular resistance against occupation. It is precisely at this stage that a reconstruction of the women's liberation formula began to take place; it was now evident that the formula had to take into consideration other contradictions dominating women's lives. Once this reformulation took place, the progressive women's committees' movement adopted a platform demanding simultaneous improvement in women's status, politically, economically, socially and culturally, and their liberation from all forms of exploitation.[8]

While this new formula proved an effective alternative to the traditional, charitable mode of operation (although the other continues to exist) it nevertheless fell straight into another difficulty. The problem is the imbalance among the various components of the women's liberation formula. The progressive women's committees' movement's attempts to deal with the three contradictions that subjugate Palestinian women led to the national political struggle being afforded supremacy and to the other contradictions being relegated to secondary positions. Although the conceptual framework espoused by the progressive women's movement takes these problems into consideration, the movement's practices reflect the two-stage revolution theory: national liberation now and women's liberation later appears to be the working formula rather than the consciousness presupposed by the improved women's liberation formula. These practices reflect negatively on more than one aspect of the Palestinian women's struggle. For example, the many attempts to concentrate the women's committees' efforts on specific women's issues, as opposed to the general needs and aspirations of Palestinian society, have failed. Moreover, the debate on women's issues hardly deals with those problems arising from particular economic relations between men and women and the division of labour in all its ideological, social and legal ramifications.

The problem is compounded further by the organizational nature of the committees' movement. Four such committee groups exist today in the Occupied Territories. These represent the four most important Palestinian ideological political streams, at a time when all parties concerned admit the necessity of developing a united women's front to simultaneously deal with the gender and national questions. The relationships among these women's committees is also structured and restricted by competition over such matters as which committee claims the largest number of women in its ranks; and which has succeeded in establishing the largest number of programmes for women in the largest number of villages and refugee camps in the shortest period of time. The quality of programmes is not of much concern. The problems of women have been reduced to serve the interests of thoroughly secondary, and possibly very petty, struggles between political factions, at the expense of the women of course. This phenomenon, too, reflects the problematic condition in which Palestinians, including those living under occupation, have found themselves since the early 1980s. The problematic condition, in turn, is partly the result of certain groups' attempts to achieve hegemony over political activities, including developmental and popular institutions and organizations, in the area.

Despite these difficulties, the progressive committees' movement did succeed in achieving general and feminist gain that must not be underestimated. But it remains in need of proving that it is capable of establishing and operating projects for women that focus on the particular problems of women without being overridden by an incessant desire to achieve factional political gains. Although the progressive women's committees are busy providing such basic services to women as literacy training, nursery schools, and other training projects, it still appears that the primary moving force behind these operations is the desire to gain popular support to buttress each group's position as a national/ideological political force. In the end, what defines the method of operation is the need of the national factions of men and women to assert their position within the Palestinian balance of power, rather than the needs of the women themselves. Consequently, cases of entry of more than one women's committee into a village 'to help women in solving their problems' have repeatedly sparked rivalries that are not exactly in the best interests of either women or Palestinians in general.

The importance of mass mobilization based on national political lines cannot be overemphasized. But the problem is one of providing a balance between national aims and aspirations on the one hand and the creation of a more equitable social order on the other. The difficulty of the Palestinian predicament must not be neglected either; for the convoluted Palestinian political map is bound to present the women's movement with serious problems. Yet if there is a lesson to be learned from other women's liberation movements — such as that of Algerian women, which suffered a substantial setback after national liberation — it is the necessity of uniting theory and practice. The danger in the present strategy for women's liberation is that an exclusive emphasis on the national question now might make it impossible to adequately address other contradictions later.

In summary, then, the reality of the lives of refugee camp and rural women in the Israeli Occupied Territories demands a re-examination and reassessment of the two stage revolution strategy by the progressive women's movement, and of the practices that necessarily stem from the adoption of that strategy. The evidence available so far points to the need to approach the analysis of women's issues with caution, and with great flexibility. It also indicates that the reality in which women live stems from the interaction of the problems resulting from the national struggle with other conflicts that are generated internally, that is, economic and social conflicts between men and women that are a result of an inequitable Palestinian social order existing prior to military rule. These influences have led to significant social changes, some affecting all the women of the Occupied Territories, and others influencing only a particular sector and in uneven ways. The sum of these interactions between military rule, and class and gender conflicts presents a paradoxical reality: the national question is a major factor which both supports the movement for women's liberation and simultaneously limits its further development. It supports liberation by calling on women to move beyond the household realm and to face the occupation (side by side) with men. But it deters further development by emptying it of its feminist and class content and limiting it to the confines of the national liberation struggle. This, in turn, impedes the development of a feminist strategy independent of, yet integrally linked to, the national struggle.

The lives of Palestinian women living under Israeli military rule are governed by various forces affecting their lives in differing ways. This necessitates a flexibility when analysing women's problems that is able to reflect the balance between the forces that ultimately determine actual conditions. One of the ways of conveying the elements of such a reality is to reconstruct the profiles of some of the personalities that have been encountered and are thought to best capture the essence of the predicament of Palestinian women. Following are two such profiles reproduced taking into primary consideration these women's own consciousness.

Umm Rukaya

Rukaya was one of the young women chosen by the village committee to help us in a health survey we were conducting in this village of about 3,000 people. Initially, eight women from the village volunteered for the task, but as the home visits progressed, four were forced to withdraw as a result of the pressure imposed on them by male relatives. The father, brother or even sometimes distant male relatives opposed the idea that unmarried women would move from house to house, leaving their *hamula's* (extended family or clan) quarters and venturing into other *haras* (quarters). For, after all, 'virtuous women ought to confine themselves to their houses and *haras'* except on the occasion of formal visits — such movements are accompanied by male relatives or older women chaperons.

The four women who remained working with us, including Rukaya, were not spared criticisms or opposition either. But they possessed the necessary resilience to withstand the pressures of resistance to the new role they were playing. They were armed with the backing and full support of the newly emerging women's committees' movement that was calling for the equal participation of Palestinian women in political economic, social and cultural life. One of the committees had just taken root in the village, adding fuel to the already existing fire of change.

Rukaya's family was one of the poorest in the village. Her father, a politically aware and apparently socially conscious man was a wage-labourer who worked in construction. He worked primarily in Israel and occasionally — depending on the availability of work — in the settlements that were being erected around his village. The village was situated just at the Green Line — the imaginary divide that separated the West Bank from Israel before 1967 — and, therefore, constituted an important strategic and political spot. Thus hundreds of village dunums were confiscated, forcing the men and male children of the village to seek work opportunities in Israel, or in building the settlements that were being erected on the very agricultural land stolen from them and that previously had been their major source of livelihood. Rukaya's father was in this category of workers, who no longer had a fixed source of income. He was paid only if he worked that day. His family was left without income on holidays, when he fell sick, or on the days of national uprising and general strikes. Two of his teenage sons were also wage workers, having left school at an early age to help their father in making ends meet.

Rukaya, too, was forced to leave school at the age of 12, but for a different reason: she suffered from repeated attacks of asthma leading to her hospitalization on several occasions. By the time she had recovered she lost interest in repeating the year at school. Thus she ended up spending her days at home, helping her mother with the daily chores and taking care of her baby sister Yassar (meaning 'left' in Arabic) until we found her.

Umm Rukaya (Rukaya's mother), like hundreds of other women in her village who have experienced numerous pregnancies, looks much older than her real age. Her sun-tanned face, her ever-tired eyes and what was left of her teeth, bear concrete evidence of her poor health , and the difficult life she must have led. She was barely 40 years old and her youngest child, Yassar, was eleven months-old.

Yassar's birth was more difficult than all of Umm Rukaya's other births. A caesarean section was urgently needed and Umm Rukaya thus decided not to have any more children. Yet, despite this decision, she failed to return to the hospital for the tubal ligation that was deemed necessary by her gynaecologist. He had already warned that her consecutive pregnancies had compromised her health sufficiently to warrant immediate and effective action. Instead of the tubal ligation, deemed too radical by her husband (although available free of charge) she arranged with him to put aside a sum of money for an IUD insertion at a private clinic. But when the money became available Umm Rukaya was faced with a dilemma. Her eldest daughter, married at the age of 14 to a man 20 years her senior, needed an IUD inserted immediately and had no money to pay for it. She already had five children and her wage-worker husband lay in bed sick most of the year. Naturally Umm Rukaya felt she had no choice and did not hesitate: she gave her daughter the money that was put aside to save herself with. To her, a woman in her 20s was much more likely to become pregnant without contraceptive protection that a woman of 40.

Several months later the half-expected happened, and Umm Rukaya, pregnant, went to seek an abortion at a clinic. But she was firmly told that her condition required no less than the care and facilities of a bona fide hospital. The news struck her like lightning and she suddenly began to fear for her life. She felt cornered, frustrated and afraid, having tried with failure every possible concoction and indigenous medical recipe said to guarantee quick and effective abortion. Carrying heavy weights did not work, nor did jumping off high places. Even drinking and eating the herbs that were well known to cause heavy bleeding in the most resilient cases did not work either. Umm Rukaya was thus in total despair.

Abu Rukaya (Rukaya's father) was uneasy and anxious. He wanted the abortion performed as soon as possible, but did not want to pay for it. He thus sought our help, along with his wife. We arranged for the procedure quickly, in view of Umm Rukaya's deteriorating health. The process, however, required that the family would pay for half the costs. But Abu Rukaya refused to pay even a small portion of the cost, although it was clear that he could afford to contribute from his own money. It eventually transpired that what mattered primarily to him was that he would be spared spending anything from his own pocket, for such an expenditure on his wife was clearly not worth it. He consoled and justified himself to us by saying that: 'My wife is as strong as a horse. In previous pregnancies, she used to suffer and lose weight, but only during the first couple of months. Then she would recover and deliver without major problems. So she can certainly withstand another pregnancy and delivery.'

Thus we left Umm Rukaya, well into her fourth month of pregnancy, showing signs of great fatigue, even exhaustion, on her face. Will her husband be satisfied when she finally gives birth? Will he be willing for her to have a tubal ligation? Or will she remain in his eyes 'as strong as a horse', capable of going through yet another pregnancy? Will he eventually consent and give her the 'green light' to avoid another mistake?

Umm Salameh

We found Umm Salameh (the mother of Salameh) by the *taboun* (local traditional oven). She was busy trying to do two things at once: bake her bread and gossip with the group of women waiting their turn to use the oven. *Tabouns* are shared by a few households that are usually related by blood or marriage, and to a lesser extent by neighbours. There are many good reasons for sharing a *taboun*. To begin with, its capacity generally exceeds the average daily needs of one family. It is, in addition, completely handmade from a mixture of clay, hay, stones and other materials that are found naturally. But it also requires a substantial amount of maintenance, and sharing reduces the workload needed (a woman's responsibility, of course). Sharing its fuel — a mixture of firewood, dried leaves and animal manure — reduces the costs as well. Yet the unintended consequence of *taboun* sharing of importance to women is that baking bread is one of the few times when women can legitimately meet other women and socialize during the working day. Though many women visit each other's homes during the late afternoons, some are denied these opportunities by their husbands, mothers-in-law or fathers. Baking bread, as is the case with water collection from the spring, provides those women with the necessary legitimacy for contact with others. While working on the land provides an outlet for socializing, it is seasonal, rather than daily in nature. Furthermore, it does not lend itself to the type of extended social sessions that occur by the *taboun* because of the nature of the work being performed.

Umm Salameh's face was flushed by the heat of both the fire and the discussion. The topic of that day was the '*leshka* women' (*leshka* is a Hebrew word that has been adapted into Arabic among some Palestinian communities that denotes the Israeli Bureau of Employment of Palestinian Arab workers from the Israeli occupied territories), the phenomenon of village women wage-workers in Israel. According to Umm Salameh, the *leshka* women were mostly agricultural labourers:

> Along with children, and God forbid, with men, they leave their homes in the early morning hours before sunrise, and, imagine, in the dark. They are transported into Israeli farms by way of special Israeli trucks [intended to facilitate the transport of workers from the territories' villages into Israel]. They return, once again, in the dark and in the company of men. They return carrying vegetables and fruits that have been obtained from the farms where they work, and feed them to their families.

All the women labourers of the region, according to the *taboun* sessions-holders, came from refugee camps. The women incessantly denied the existence of women workers in Israel who originated in the village or nearby villages. They insisted that this phenomenon was restricted to refugee camps, and that village folk would never allow such a thing to happen to their women and daughters. Umm Salameh summed up the collective position regarding women and wage labour by saying '*ihna ma 'ndnash niswan bitishtghel*' (we do not have women that work).

An apparently significant stigma was attached to wage labour among women, especially if they sought work in Israel. The reasons were, in part, spelled out by one of the participants in the discussion:

> The *leshka* women behave in a loose and immoral way. Going away from the village to work means meeting strange men, and having to deal with them and to keep their company. It also means coming back home in the dark, unaccompanied . . . All these excessive liberties are bound to make a weak woman go astray . . . I tell you, they end up behaving in a very immoral way. Look at what happened when one of the *leshka* women from the nearby refugee camp came to visit our village. She was standing in the street, talking with other women. A young and handsome donkey rider was passing by. She must have fancied him. So she ran towards him and jumped on the back of the donkey and circled her arms around the rider's waist. Do you call that moral behaviour?

But there is at least one more reason for the stigma attached to women's wage labour that was not spelt out by the participants. In Palestinian culture, women and children, the 'weaker sector of society', are seen as the responsibility of men. The obligations of men towards women are varied, but one important obligation is the provision of an adequate income. This holds true even in peasant villages that rely on agriculture as a primary source of income, and where women participate to a considerable extent in working the land. Despite women's work on the family farm, the financial aspects of the operation and the ultimate responsibility for the family's income is a man's domain. When a woman leaves her house or her village in search of paid work, it is seen as an indication that the male household members can no longer provide an income sufficient to fulfil their family's needs. Otherwise, why would the men allow the women to work? And this, to the villagers, is a source of shame, not only to the woman's husband and in-laws, but also to her parents.

Umm Salameh's posture reflected her economic and social position in the village. She was the wife, and the only wife, of one of the two Mukhtars (clan or extended family head) of the village. This fact was also reflected in her confidence, eloquence and general attitude towards other women, and ourselves. She came from a well-to-do background and had married into a landed and notable family. All her male children were abroad, working in the Arabian Gulf. They were well-educated, she boasted, and held important technical positions. One of her sons had just left the village the year before. He went to work with his brothers, leaving his young wife and two male children under her care. Her house was full of the evidence of remittance money: spaciousness, electrical gadgets, even a private internal piped water supply that is connected to an electric pump. It seemed as if they were all arranged for display, as status symbols, rather than for use. Pictures of migrants were hung everywhere, as stark reminders of the price of separation families must pay for this newly generated source of wealth. Yet despite all this Umm Salameh still possessed an unbreakable attachment to the land. She was Mother Earth herself.

She showed us some of the family land that she herself tilled. All she grew was used for family consumption, not for sale. No, they did not need that source of food, but the land had to be tilled, to keep the tradition alive. Most of the family land has not been tilled for years now. The children were away and the father was too old to work it himself or oversee the work by paid labourers. Even their olive trees were being neglected, and this fact was a source of worry and deep concern for her. She seemed of two minds over the issue. On the one hand, she approved of migration because of all the new opportunities it brought to her family. Despite the separation in her mind, the bond between the family members was not weakened but strengthened, especially among the brothers. On the other hand, the increasing difficulties that she and her husband were facing in tilling the land, and its neglect as a result of her sons' departure was becoming a very worrisome and almost unbearable thought. Umm Salameh was caught between two worlds with different values. In the end, it appeared as if she were accepting the present and parting with the past. She consoled herself with the thought that, after all, it would have been very difficult for all her sons to make a good living had they stayed in the village. She also consoled herself with the idea that at least her sons were working in Arab countries and in 'respectable non-manual' jobs, unlike many other men from the nearby village, who were well-educated but were forced by circumstances to work in Israel as wage labourers.

Notes

1. Look at, for instance, Bendt, I. and Downing, J., *We Shall Return, Women of Palestine*, Zed Press, London, 1982. Haddad, Y., 'Palestinian Women: Patterns of Legitimation and Domination' in Nakhleh, K. and Zureik, E., *The Sociology of the Palestinians*, Croom Helm, London, 1980, pp. 147–75, and Peteet, J., *Women and the Palestinian Movement, No Going Back?*, MERIP No. 138, January–February 1986, pp. 20–24.

2. Al-Khalili, G., *al-Mar'a al-Falastinia Wa al-Thawra*, Dar al-Aswar, Akkar, 1981, p. 70 (in Arabic).

3. The information in this section has been obtained from several sources including discussions and interviews the authors had with selected leaders of the women's movement of the time. Interestingly, some of the women's activities of the late 1940s were documented in the form of reports that these women's societies wrote about their work. An example of such reports is that published by the Arab Women's Union of Bethlehem by Jacir, N., *Communiqué of the Arab Women's Union, Its Two First Aid Stations and Activities*, 1947–50, Jerusalem, 1950 (in Arabic).

4. al-Khalili, op. cit., pp. 77–81.

5. Even in the early 1980s, in local newspapers one of the women's societies advertised presents and trophies for those Palestinian women who have had more than ten children!

6. See, for instance, Dakkak, I., 'Back to Square One: A Study in the Reemergence of the Palestinian Identity in the West Bank 1967–1980' in Schoelch, A. (ed.), *Palestinians Over the Green Line*, Ithaca, London, 1983.

7. This information is based on discussion that took place over the years between the authors and selected leaders of the committees' movement, especially those belonging to the Women's Work Committees and the Working Women's Committees. They are also based on personal experience and a work relationship between the authors and members of this movement that dates back to the movement's inception.

8. See, for instance, The Women's Work Committees, *Tarik al-Mar'a* (the Road of the Woman), Ramallah, March, 1982 (in Arabic), Working Women's Committees, *Bulletin of Palestinian Working Women's Union in the West Bank and Gaza Strip*, Jerusalem, August 1983 and Women's Work Committees, *Women's Work Committees in the Occupied Territories, Bulletin for December 1983*, Jerusalem, January–February 1984.

6. United Nations Resolutions and Instruments Concerning Women

Mervat El Tillawi

Introduction

The Preamble to the United Nations Charter expresses the determination of all peoples to 'save succeeding generations from the scourge of war', and

> to reaffirm faith in fundamental rights, in the dignity and worth of the human person, in the equal rights of men and women and of nations large and small, to establish conditions under which justice and respect for the obligations arising from treaties and other sources of international law can be maintained . . . [and] . . . to employ international machinery for the promotion of the economic and social advancement of all peoples.

Such was the commitment of those states which were signatories of the United Nations Charter; they guaranteed equal rights between men and women as well as between nations. Further, the determination to employ an international organization as a means to promote the advancement of peoples necessarily requires that its resolutions and recommendations are respected.

After a lengthy period international organizations represented by the United Nations attained legal recognition by states. Their legal status had been developing since the mid-19th century along with international law, for the purpose of bringing order to the increasing interrelations between states.

International organizations thus acquired the status of an international legal individual, with the same duties, responsibilities and rights, and were entitled to enter into contractual agreements. According to Article 104 of the Charter, member states granted the international organizations due legal competence to exercise their activities within the territories of states; further, such international organizations have the right to appeal to the International Court of Justice, and to maintain ships flying its flag. As a result of the development of this legal status, the study of organizations came into being. Organizations issued their own publications and studies, and set rules of procedure. Thus the function of international officer emerged, international conventions were signed and the importance of ensuring conformity between national legislation and international conventions was emphasized. Various bodies and departments came to be established in member states to co-operate with the international organizations.

Implementation of the resolutions and decisions of international organizations is primarily the responsibility of member states. Implementation is, however, a matter that falls within the realm of state sovereignty, and for this reason it is important to answer the question that is often raised these days related to the significance of such resolutions and the doubts about the effectiveness of international organizations.

In so far as the issue of women in the United Nations is concerned it will be seen that a great deal has been done, but implementation remains entirely in the hands of member states. The real strength of any organization, no doubt, depends on the determination and will of its members.

The issue of women in the United Nations

Since its inception, the United Nations has been concerned with the issue of women. This interest has been as a result of its awareness that the development of human societies, and their changing conditions throughout history, have affected the status of women both negatively and positively.

Two main UN organs, the General Assembly and the Economic and Social Council (which is responsible for the recommendations and resolutions of the Commission on the Status of Women of the United Nations) alone have issued 366 resolutions in the last 40 years. This figure does not include the recommendations and resolutions of specialized agencies and of other United Nations' organs.

Table 6.1 shows the resolutions taken on women's status and their dates of issue; table 6.2 indicates the subjects and the percentage of their distribution since the beginning of the Decade of Women.

Table 6.1
Recommendations and resolutions

Organ	*1946–55*	*1956–65*	*1966–75*	*1976–85*	*Total*
General Assembly	12	13	30	111	166
Economic & Social Council	15	10	68	107	200
Total	*27*	*23*	*98*	*218*	*366*

Table 6.2
Subjects and percentage distribution of Resolutions adopted since the beginning of the Decade of Women

Subject	*%*		
Equality	15.8	Regional & international co-operation	12.3
Development	15.8	General	32.7
Peace	8.1	Commission on Women	8.8
Private sectors	6.3		

Source: Paper prepared by the Centre for Women, Vienna

Concern for women's affairs extended over three phases. The first started in 1946, and for the following 20 years focused on promulgating legislation and codifying social and human relations. Hence, during this phase the UN concentrated on the study of the status of women within the framework of human rights, and issued a number of international instruments pertaining to the rights of women in political, economic and social fields, the latter also related to children (see appendix 1).

It should be noted in this respect that the Declaration for the Protection of Women and Children in Emergency and Armed Conflicts was the result of Arab women's experience under Israeli occupation and due to initiatives of Egypt's representative. Her endeavours were aimed at drawing the international community's attention to the inhuman conditions under which women and children exist in times of war and armed conflict. Such initiatives were staunchly opposed at the outset by Western states, on the pretext that they implied the politicization of meetings dedicated to women. The truth, however, was soon revealed, precisely that humanitarian legislation was conceived on the assumption that the Second World War was to be the last war in history, hence no adequate legislation for the protection of the civil population was promulgated. Participating states unanimously supported the initiative and adopted the Universal Declaration to be binding on all. The initiative reaped further success in so far as it drew the attention of other United Nations organs to the need to close the gap in international law for the protection of all civilians in times of war. Two protocols were issued in Geneva in 1977 for this purpose.

The second phase witnessed the shift from codification to implementation, giving effect to the principles and rights enshrined in international conventions. More interest was shown in the problems facing women in their everyday lives; a programme of advisory services and fellowships for training women and enhancing their skills was also adopted.

The effectiveness of such programmes was, however, limited, partly due to the enormous number of women in urgent need of effective improvement of their status, and to lack of political will and the sharp disparity in the status of women from one country to another and from rural to urban areas in the same country. Women live under varying conditions, have different requirements depending on their levels of education, type of work, social conditions, and so on. The common denominator, however, is the inequality and discrimination they face.

The third phase in the United Nations action for raising awareness for the cause of women and for the need to improve their conditions, particularly in developing countries, was the declaration of the International Year for Women, and the designation of the years 1975–85 as the International Decade for Women. These measures aimed to bring to world public opinion the critical issues relating to women viewed from a new perspective, precisely, that they were issues of concern not only to women but to the entire society. Women constitute 50% of human resources, hence may not be denied adequate planning and training to help them to participate effectively in social, economic and political development as well as raise their status.

Achievements

In addition to recommendations and resolutions adopted, the United Nations took the following positive measures to improve the standard of conditions of women:

1. Established international machinery to supervise the implementation of conventions; the latest convention for the Elimination of All Forms of Discrimination Against Women was issued in 1979. At the Second Conference on Women, held in Copenhagen in 1980, 87 states signed the Convention which came into force in March 1981.

2. Established a committee within the framework of the United Nations to supervise the implementation of the provisions of the Convention by reviewing periodical reports presented by states. The committee is composed of 23 experts from various countries (one of whom is an Egyptian) who operate in their personal capacities. The members are selected by states which are parties to the Convention and the term of office is four years, open to extension. The Committee holds annual meetings in New York or Vienna.

3. Approved the principle of receiving complaints from individuals; any individual who is suffering due to their government's contravention of the principle of equality, is entitled to complain to the UN Committee on the Status of Women and the UN will raise the issue with the government concerned.

4. Set up a fund to finance and promote the establishment of women's productive projects in various countries. Since its establishment at the outset of the International Decade of Women the fund has assisted in setting up more than 400 projects in 80 countries. Several projects have been funded in the Arab region whether through the Economic Committee for West Asia (ECWA), which comprises 14 Arab states, or through Arab governments directly.

5. During the International Decade for Women, the UN established the International Institute for Research and Training for women. The main focus of the Institute is to undertake studies and research and to provide statistics and information concerning the role of women in development. The training programmes offered by the Institute deal with the different sectors and aspects of development which have not received adequate attention in the past.

The Institute has published a series of studies on the role of women in commerce, agriculture, technology, industry, money and finance. A number of Arab women participated in the operation of the Institute by presiding over the preparatory committee which drew up its Statutes, became members of its board of directors (from Egypt and Morocco) and managed its department of research and training.

6. The Secretariat of the UN Committee on the Status of Women, with headquarters in Vienna, is the main UN organ responsible for follow-up of the implementation of resolutions and recommendations adopted by the international organization. The Secretariat receives the replies of states and evaluates the state of implementation of work, plans, and strategies relevant to

women. As the competent organ to prepare for international meetings on women, it is in constant touch with member states with regard to activities aiming to improve womens' conditions. One of the highest posts in the Secretariat is occupied by an Algerian woman.

7. Since the Mexico Program of Action was issued in 1975, and the declaration of the Decade of Women, various UN organs and specialized agencies established offices, departments or internal units to deal with topics related to women and to co-ordinate their activities with those of other organs of the United Nations. In establishing such offices, the aim is to ensure that programmes for the promotion of women are integrated in the work plans of such organs and agencies in compliance with the resolutions of the UN calling for the integration of women in all phases of development.

8. The five regional economic committees of the United Nations co-ordinate and co-operate with governments and regional governmental organizations in the different geographical areas in following up the status of women, and in designing plans and programmes for the advancement of women in their respective regions. The five committees played an effective role in preparing for the three international conferences held for the promotion of women. The vitality of these committees has motivated many governments to provide information on the status of women in the various fields of activity which, in previous years, had not been available. Particular mention should be made of ECWA for the efforts it is launching to improve the status of women in the Arab countries' members in the Committee.

9. The United Nations requested governments to establish committees or other national organs to act as focal points for co-ordinating national bodies concerned with women with the United Nations, in order to ensure implementation of the resolutions and work plans adopted by international conferences. Many states have already established such national bodies for the follow-up of the implementation of women's programmes. A UN study revealed, however, that while some of these bodies were functioning efficiently, a considerable number needed financial support.

Constraints

A review of progress achieved may give the false impression that women's problems have been solved. But women still face many obstacles which vary according to the level of socio-economic development achieved by the society in question. Evaluation of the status of women undertaken prior to the Nairobi conference revealed the following:

1. Despite the fact that most constitutions provide for equality between the sexes, discrimination against women persisted in practical life. In other words, disparity is apparent between the provisions of law and its implementation. The main obstacles to the implementation of law may be summarized as follows:

a) Lack of a strong administrative system in most developing countries capable of monitoring the enforcement of law;

b) Misinterpretation of law due to the persisting influence of customs and traditions that affect life styles and modes of thinking.

c) Women's ignorance of their rights due to their ignorance of the law.

d) Failure to periodically revise laws and regulations in order to ensure that consistency with developments taking place in the society is maintained.

2. Despite the enormous progress achieved in the field of education, the process of socialization and the indoctrination of youth with obsolete ideas related to a division of labour between the sexes or fixed roles, helps perpetuate discrimination against women. In addition, socialization affects women's concept of themselves and the value of their role in society. Furthermore, women have no real idea of their potentials.

3. The definition of work as waged labour has rendered women's work – whether in the household, the fields or any kind of work to serve the husband or the family – as unwaged and consequently not recognized as work. Women's work is, therefore, not valued. To aggravate the situation further, women's fertility is itself held against them.

4. In training and job opportunities and for scholarships, preference is given to males on the pretext that men, and not women, are the providers for the family. This, however, is a gross error as 30% of families in the majority of societies are supported by women.

5. Women are persistently reluctant to participate in political life in the belief that politics is for men only. Organizations to stimulate and encourage women to exercise their political rights are absent.

6. Persistent high illiteracy rates and even their increase in certain geographical areas.

After forty years: analysis of main developments

The recommendations of the United Nations incorporated in work plans and strategies at the Mexico, Copenhagen and Nairobi meetings have revealed the correlation between the failure to grant women equality and the socio-economic conditions prevailing in these societies, or rather in the international community at large. The world economic crisis has its repercussions on the economies of developing countries, in addition, political instability is unfavourable to economic growth.

The approach to the question of women should take into account women's role in the development process. Theories and concepts of development, revised in the light of the experience of the United Nations and of the developing countries, have proved the fallacy of the realization of economic development in isolation from social and political dimensions.

Similarly, concepts of development have undergone a change. While, in the past, the objectives of development focused on quantified criteria and index figures, disregarding other aspects involved, the focus today is on progressive improvement of living standards of a people, on the basis of full participation in the development effort and equal distribution of the resulting benefits, as prescribed by the UN Strategy for the Third Development Decade. Hence, we may conclude that economic growth, productive labour and social justice are basic, correlated factors for development.

The approach to the question of women has, therefore, become dominated by the new insight related to women's role in development, and the early 1970s witnessed lengthy discussions in international fora on the designation and concept, which subsequently underwent several stages in its evolution to the present.

The first stage is characterized by the attitude of developed countries which viewed the women's case as merely one of providing welfare programmes unrelated to development plans and projects. Women's programmes thus remained marginal; isolated from the process of social or economic development. In the second stage, programmes were designed for the purpose of raising women's incomes. Consequently, foreign aid to developing countries from donor countries and international organizations took the form of activities which generated income for women, but remained tied to foreign assistance or financing which, if discontinued for any reason, would bring the whole project to a standstill. Projects of this kind employed a limited number of women and operated in such restricted areas as community services and crafts. Evaluation of projects established during this stage revealed that they failed to serve the desired objective, namely, the integration of women and their effective contribution in the realization of socio-economic development on the large scale targeted. Evaluation also revealed the absence of solutions to the problems of rural women and of women in the poorer urban areas.

It, therefore, became necessary to urge that women's role and their fuller integration in development be reviewed. This approach was first called for by women in the developing countries who were actually participating in the development process during their daily work; tilling the land, carrying water pots, collecting wood for fuel and walking long distances to market-places to buy or sell their produce, in addition to other agricultural-based activities and domestic work. The question is inevitably asked, what more can women offer to the development process? The answer is that women should receive their share of the benefits of development. According to ILO statistics: *women comprise ½ the population; represent ⅓ of the total labour force; work ⅔ of all working hours; receive ¹/₁₀ of gross income; and own ¹/₁₀₀ of world property.*

These figures reveal that women do participate effectively in development, but their labour and contribution is neither visible, recognized, appreciated, nor assessed by economic systems. Such systems restrict their recognition to those economic activities in terms of which wages are allocated to each worker.

In Egypt for example, official statistics indicate that women constitute 14% of the labour force. This percentage excludes rural women whose labour is free since they receive no wages from husband or household members for their work on the fields. The figure may, therefore, be considered as incorrect.

Such developments led to the third stage characterized by the search for a development strategy, the determination of methods for its implementation and the definition of its objectives. The development strategies adopted during the three previous decades, varying from economic growth to import substitution and to the promotion of exports, were widely discussed. It was observed that the numerous development schemes adopted had failed to distribute the benefits to the various sectors of the population participating, and this led to deteriorating conditions for certain of these sectors, the majority of which comprised women.

A further example is that of African women in the south Sahara region, who perform 80% of agricultural work – in addition to their other roles. Women's burdens are further increased by the imposition of agricultural policies which encourage export products such as wheat, maize, and so on, with the aim of obtaining foreign currrency. Such policies helped to convert the village from a productive to a consumptive unit, thus aggravating the problems of food supplies and creating dependence on food imports. Such agricultural policies had grave implications for women, making their task of supplying food for the family more difficult; this, in many cases, induced women to migrate to urban centres, only to add to the already serious problems in those areas.

Developing countries are profoundly affected by the fluctuating world economic situation to which they are closely tied. Transnational corporations and multinational companies that dominate the world economic system today have created an international division of labour and assimilated a large proportion of the world market for goods and services. Both these facts have had adverse implications for the status of women in many developing countries. An example of this policy is the creation of free commercial zones. Industries established in these zones could provide women with opportunities for work in textile, electronic, food industries and the like. But the fleeting nature of such investments, ever seeking higher returns and turning to those developing countries that offer the most favourable conditions to foreign capital, made these job opportunities for women transient and unstable.

For these reasons, the issue of women and development should be treated from an overall perspective. Fragmentary or marginal approaches to women's issues in isolation from socio-economic development plans have led to superficial solutions which only drain the already meagre resources of developing countries which, if used properly, could have brought them closer to their goals. Statistics and data about women's true role in the social, economic and cultural fields should be made accessible to decision makers and development scheme designers in order to ensure that development plans meet the real needs of women.

Developing countries' problems are becoming more complex and diversified. It is essential that an integrated indigenous policy which takes account of the peculiar economic and cultural conditions of the society is sought. Emulating theories that proved successful in other countries can exacerbate problems and prove to be a total failure. Similarly, reliance on foreign assistance may conflict with national development plans. United Nations statistics revealed that the greater part of investments in developing countries are from the savings of their respective nationals rather than from foreign investments. In the event of approval of foreign assistance, these funds should be used to complete development projects determined in the light of the needs and priorities conceived by each country.

In formulating a development policy, care should be taken not to turn development into a threat to society particularly to the poorer classes and more specifically to women who are, (according to UN statistics), the poorest among the poor. Self-reliance should be enhanced both at the individual and national level while dependency and charity should be strictly unacceptable since other parties will always seek to share in the benefits reaped.

After Nairobi, what?

New insight into women's issues resulted from the preparatory work for the Decade for Women, and from the general interest generated in various countries and groupings concerned with related matters. Similarly, research undertaken within the context of numerous meetings helped to define standpoints and attitudes towards issues which had been the subject of a great deal of argument in the past.

These insights revealed that women's issues do not pertain to women alone, but concern the society as a whole. For this reason previous attempts to deal with women's problems from a social welfare point of view have failed because women's problems must be treated within the overall development process, as they are part of the productive force and an essential beneficiary from development.

In view of the heavy burden placed on the shoulders of governments, women's associations and federations should face up to their responsibilities and collaborate to enhance the status of women. They should design comprehensive programmes which promote both urban and rural women, and advocate policies to render women's role more effective in the realization of socio-economic development. Women should also change their self-image and that of their role in the family and in society at large. They should become aware of their potential and that their unity could constitute a powerful force.

Appendix

- Convention for the Suppression of the Traffic in Persons and of the Exploitation of the Prostitution of Others (1949).
- Convention on the Political Rights of Women (1952).
- Convention on Consent to Marriage, Minimum Age for Marriage and Registration of Marriages (1962).
- Convention on the Nationality of Married Women (1957).

- Declaration on the Elimination of Discrimination Against Women (1967).
- Declaration on the Protection of Women and Children in Emergency and Armed Conflicts (1974).
- Convention on the Elimination of All Forms of Discrimination against Women (1979).

7. The Legal Status of Palestinian Women in the Occupied Territories

Mona Rishmawi

Introduction

Anyone who researches issues relating to women inevitably encounters the degree to which these issues are intertwined with the historical, political, economic and legal experiences of the people in the place of research. From the start, the researcher will realize that to separate the experience of a certain sector of the people from the factors that did and do influence the history of that people is impossible.

Similarly, researchers working on any subject related to the Palestinians must confront their past and present uprooting, dispersion and forced emigration. The first issue I had to deal with when trying to define the parameters of this chapter was the extent of the abiding effect of the disaster of 1948 upon the Palestinian people and its particular effects upon Palestinian women.

Until 1948 and the diaspora, Palestinians were united by a common national history. Since 1948, however, individual women's experiences differ according to the various geographical locations: the West Bank, the Gaza Strip, the area declared the 'State of Israel', Lebanon, Syria, Egypt, Jordan, or any other Arab or foreign country. These varied experiences made it necessary to select one locale; I accordingly chose the West Bank, because of my personal familiarity with it and my study of the situation and the laws here. The other areas where Palestinians live, inside or outside Palestine, are not, therefore, addressed here.

I propose here to focus on collective, organized women's movements and work, since I believe that the strongest guarantee of strengthening women's position in any given society is the existence of a vital movement which places women's rights and freedoms among its national priorities of liberation, progress and the exercise of basic rights and freedoms.

The Palestinian women's movement can be traced to the beginning of the 20th century. When the Palestinians mobilized to meet the pressing need to establish both their Palestinian and Arab identity, Palestinian women were in the front ranks. This was clearly the case in the British Mandate period, and their involvement under the current Israeli occupation is even stronger. In Mandate times, however, the Palestinian women's movement played a supporting role to the national struggle, and did not include specific women's rights among its stated goals; today, in contrast, there is a popular women's movement encouraging the active participation of women in the struggle for their rights and freedom.

The position of Palestinian women in the West Bank greatly regressed during the Jordanian period of 1948 to 1967, perhaps because of rule by a non-Palestinian regime with particular considerations and interests. In general, the Jordanian regime failed to take into consideration the socio-historical experience and natural development of Palestinians, and to include their rights and freedoms among its priorities.

With regard to the legal context of this chapter, I have examined laws that directly affect the position of women, such as the laws of personal status and the Penal Code, and also those that indirectly affect their position, to show the laws' historic context and to link them to various social values. When dealing with the Jordanian period I have frequently compared the provisions of Jordanian law with those of other Arab states in order to support my view of the regressive values adopted by the Jordanian legislators.

This chapter makes no claim to be a complete study of the situation of Palestinian women; it can be no more than an introduction. The period from the Ottomans until the present Israeli Occupation and its relevant laws are considered in light of: 1) Assessment of the growing role played by women, and how deeply this role is rooted in Palestinian society during each of the successive historical periods. The history of the Palestinians and of other peoples who have undergone colonization demonstrates that in cases of struggles for national liberation the roles of women greatly expand, only to deteriorate when the struggle has ended; and 2) The role of the law in affecting the position of Palestinian women in each of the different historical stages. Has the law aided the development of their position or not?

Women at the beginning of the 20th century

Palestine and other Arab countries were under Ottoman rule until 1918, and after the First World War, in 1922, Palestine was officially placed under British Mandate.

Towards the end of their rule, the Ottomans had set about the codification of a set of laws in most areas of their Empire. As far as social issues and women's affairs were concerned, they had promulgated personal status laws which applied in the Arab countries, giving the religious courts authority in these matters.

In 1870 the Ottomans collected the principles of Islamic civil law and set them down in a 'code', *al-Majalla al-Adiliya*.[1] The significance of this ruling is that it was the first time the Ottomans had made use of the flexibility of Islamic law; previously they had applied only the authoritative opinion of the Hanafi school of law. In the *Majalla*, minority views of the same school were adopted in order to render the provisions more in accord with the circumstances of the time.

When in 1917 the Ottomans issued, for the first time in Islamic history, a 'code' of personal status, they did not adhere to the Hanafi school alone, but adopted provisions from other schools. They gave a woman the right to seek dissolution of her marriage on a number of grounds, including certain diseases afflicting the husband, his failure to maintain her, his absence and injury. These and other grounds were not recognized by classical Hanafi law, which was extremely restrictive on this point.

With regard to polygamy, although the law did not actually forbid it, it adopted one provision aimed at limiting it: a wife could stipulate in her marriage contract that her husband might not marry another wife while she remained married to him, and that if he did, she would be divorced. This stipulation did not render the second marriage void, but gave the previous wife the power to divorce herself should she choose to do so.

Empowered by the Mandate the British government exercised wide legislative powers. They promulgated several laws modifying and replacing various Ottoman laws, but paid little attention to the laws of personal status, particularly the legal principles that affected the position of women, which they left unchanged. The new laws recognized certain non-Muslim religious communities not previously recognized by the Ottomans, and empowered them to establish autonomous courts and apply their own laws therein.[2]

The political climate of Palestine in the Mandate period – the presence of the Mandate government itself, the increased Jewish immigration to Palestine, the spread of Zionism – put Palestinians on their guard and made them fearful for their country's future. Palestinian women – more especially those who were wives or relatives of men politically involved[3] – were stimulated to come out into the front line and urge Palestinian women to participate in the national struggle.[4]

Palestinian women were later influenced by the education boom in the Arab world during the late 19th century which resulted in the spread of schools – especially missionary institutions. The Ottoman state had opposed this development, but its weak position in the years preceding and during the First World War diminished its influence. Although the British imposed a system of compulsory education shortly after they took over in Palestine, they failed to enforce it effectively. They also encouraged missionary schools, which virtually invaded Palestine. Esma Tubi, in *Abir and Majd*, writes that parents did send their children to these schools despite their rejection of the new Western ideas and attitudes that accompanied the education they received there.

Foreign missionary schools were not the sole source of education for girls, however; this could also be obtained in the increased number of local schools throughout the country. In 1924, for example, Nabiha Nasser founded Bir Zeit School later to become Bir Zeit College and in 1976, Bir Zeit University. Studies in the school were co-educational up to the fifth primary level, and single sex thereafter. Education for girls was not confined to the cities, but Palestinian villages too, had their share of the increased facilities. In the academic year 1944–45, for example, girls attending school up to the first preparatory grade constituted 42% of all pupils, and of these 8% were in village schools.[5]

In this period, a common denominator united the numerous activities of the women: the political struggle. This was despite the fact that the women's movement placed the controversial issues of social liberation and the removal of the veil among its goals. On 26 October 1929, the first Women's Conference was held in Jerusalem and attended by about 3,000 women from the Palestinian towns of Jerusalem, Yaffa, Haifa, Nablus, Ramallah, Jenin and others. The aim of the Conference was to organize women's work in Palestine for the recovery of the homeland, and for the aid of needy families.[6]

Many charitable societies that began work at this time were influenced by the missionary philosophy and operated on the basis of good works and charity.[7] Certain others, however, were motivated, at least in part, by their stand on political and social liberation, for example the Arab Ladies Society in Jerusalem, established in 1921. This Society was distinguished by the fact that its goals were socio-political, and its membership included Muslim and Christian women on an equal basis, which was a response to the pressing need for national duty at that time, and a contrast to the many sectarian-based societies.

Among the goals of this Society was purchasing land for the families of martyrs and founding workshops for their employment. It was thus not a matter of 'charity' – rather, the society adopted the motto: 'Earn your bread by the sweat of your brow'. It also organized the collection of second-hand books and magazines to be sent to prisoners, and called for the boycott of foreign goods and for the purchase of local products. The society had a notable effect on nationalist work at this period, perhaps because of its proximity to the course of events in Jerusalem.

Women's activities at this time, however, were mainly confined to the middle classes, and the movement's vanguard comprised the wives or relatives of male activists in the political field.[8] Its social base was thus inevitably narrow.

The realities of Palestinian village life determined a special position for women in the Palestinian countryside, since they had a major role in producing village goods. The Palestinian village was self-sufficient in terms of the variety of foodstuffs it was able to produce: peasant families raised fruit trees and planted vegetables mainly for home consumption. This was in contrast to villages in other Arab lands, for example in Egypt, which in general produced one crop only, and subsequently were unable to subsist independently of the city.[9] As Rosemary Sayigh noted:

Women had as much to do as men in the family collectives, probably more. Besides normal domestic labour and childcare, it was they who dried and stored the foodstuffs on which the family would live in winter: grains, pulses, olives, olive oil, dried fruit. They tended the orchards that encircled the villages, looked after the poultry, and often worked side by side in the fields with the men. Their strength can be felt in the way their children recollect them proudly as 'peasant-mothers', working unceasingly between home and field, carrying water and gathering firewood. In everyday language, women and the home were symbolically linked: women were its basis not only through their childbearing function, but also through their economic contribution. And more than men, it was the women's job to maintain the network of social relations on which village and family solidarity depended. Their subordination in the patriarchical family, with its glorification of male heirs, was contradicted by the strong role played by women in everyday life. And though this was rare, women sometimes owned land and managed it themselves.[10]

This situation continued until the Disaster of 1948, when the dispersion and diaspora of the Palestinian people created a new reality. Palestine was divided into three parts; the West Bank, which fell under Jordanian rule, the Gaza Strip, placed under Egyptian administration, and the remainder of Palestine, in which the 'State of Israel' was declared.

The uprooting of the people deeply affected Palestinian society and its development. Palestinians in the area declared to be Israel became refugees who fled to other areas both within and beyond the borders of Palestine, leaving their lands and vocations. The peasant class fled and huddled in camps. The loss of their land, which was the basic source of income, and the contrast between camp life and village life resulted in the loss of many qualities on which village values had been based. They maintained their traditional values for as long as possible, but eventually reality dictated the need to forge new relationships based on social and political solidarity, and to forge new values.

This political and social development varied according to the refugees' class and geographical location. The middle-class and urban Palestinians, despite their connection to the land, were not solely dependent on it as a source of income. They were equipped with skills and wealth which helped them to bear the Disaster more easily, both financially, and in finding work in the communities they fled to, in so far as the political and economic conditions there would permit.

Women in the West Bank after 1948

On 24 April 1950, in the wake of the 1948 Disaster, Jordan officially annexed the West Bank to the Hashemite Kingdom and imposed the Jordanian legal system upon it.

The official justification given for this annexation was that it was the wish of the Palestinian people, and that they would thus be able to exercise their right to self-determination.[11] Economic reasons for the annexation, however, may be more convincing: Jordan is desert terrain of which a mere 13% is cultivable, and land actually under cultivation amounts to just 4%.[12] In contrast, the West Bank is mainly agricultural land, along with the existing light industry and tourism-based economies.

In general, Jordanian society was little removed from Bedouin society. The majority of its inhabitants were nomadic Bedouin groups who depended on breeding camels and grazing livestock, along with raids on the few villages scattered at the edges of the desert or in the agricultural areas. Jordan remained a semi-feudal, tribal society until after World War II, when the Hashemite

Kingdom was established on 25 May 1946. After the annexation of the West Bank, Jordan – for the first time – was linked to world economy. This led to the expansion of markets and subsequently to the shift to agriculture and tourism.[13]

Regarding the position of women in Jordanian Bedouin society, Suhair al-Tell states:

> It can be said that the status of women in Bedouin society is tied to two fundamental concepts. The first derives from . . . the belief that she is weak and in constant need of care and protection . . . It is well known that when the Bedouin talks of his children, he does not mention his daughters . . . Bedouin laws and customs have regulated all types of relationships in Bedouin society, including everything connected to women and relationships with them . . . Perhaps the most prominent issues related to women are those of marriage and honour and of felonies and crimes, with all the matters that arise from these questions. In questions of marriage it can be said that Bedouin custom does not give the Bedouin woman the opportunity of refusing or accepting her partner in life, except, that is, in rare cases relating to the individual woman's economic or social position . . . The woman's dowry goes to her father, she having no right to any of it according to Bedouin custom. In matters of divorce and polygamy, the Bedouin do not observe religious rules and restrictions; a man may marry more than four wives, while on the other hand a woman may not seek divorce even for such defects as sexual impotence. It is, however, common for the wife to be deserted in the matrimonial home, in which case she usually remains without either divorce or marriage . . . Contracts of marriage and divorce are conducted orally in the presence of witnesses. Also in traditional Bedouin society, the *idda* [waiting period] of divorce is not observed, and children naturally 'belong' to their father, so thus in the event of divorce the mother will not see them at all.
>
> Bedouin law and custom show no tolerance of offences related to honour. Death is thus the fate of any female who transgresses the rules of honour.[14]

In determining policy towards women, the Jordanian legislators were greatly influenced by Bedouin values.[15] The positions they adopted show that the different experience, status and historical background of the Palestinian women on the one hand and the Bedouin women on the other, were totally disregarded. According to the Jordanian Constitution a male monarchial system of rule is operative; the king is the head of state[16] and males hold succession to the throne;[17] the right of the vote and candidacy for public posts is also confined to males.[18] The Constitution's provision for equality of Jordanians before the law states that discrimination on the grounds of race, language or religion shall not be allowed. Discrimination on the grounds of sex is not mentioned.[19]

Thus, with regard to women, the Jordanian legislator has pursued a policy that differs from that of other Arab countries that border Palestine and where an urban/peasant society has developed: Lebanon, Syria and Egypt. Since 1953, Lebanese law, for example, has given women the right of the vote and of candidacy for public posts, while the Egyptian and Syrian legislatures provide for mandatory female representation in Parliament.

In 1951, after discussions of changes to the personal status laws in force since Ottoman times, the Jordanian Law of Family Rights (JLF), applicable to Muslims, was passed.[20] Despite the passage of 30 years and the accompanying social changes since the promulgation of Ottoman law, few reforms were embodied in the new law, and these were more suited to the requirements of Jordanian society. In terms of polygamy, for example, the law limited the number of wives to four, since in Jordanian Bedouin society it had been possible to exceed the Islamic limit of four. The law also required the official registration of marriage and divorce, since as Suhair al-Tell stated, marriage contracts in Jordanian society had been oral only. The law did, however, widen the stipulations which a wife might put in her contract of marriage – she could, for example, now stipulate that she wanted to live in a certain town. She might still stipulate that her husband should not take another wife while married to her – this remained as it had been in Ottoman times. The second marriage was not voided, and the wife who had made the stipulation was left with the choice of either seeking dissolution for the breach of the condition, or else staying with her husband.[21]

In treating the concept of honour in the Penal code, the Jordanian legislator adopted the sternly patriarchal concepts of the Bedouin; the honour of the family springs from the honour of its women. In a recent judgement, for example, the Court of Cassation (the highest court in Jordan) pronounced:

> The award for the amount of damage which has befallen the victim's guardian through the assault upon his daughter, through which she suffered both mental and material injury and damage to his honour and dignity and to his standing among the people; is in accordance with the provisions of the law.[22]

A rapist and assaulter of honour may have his penalty waived if he marries his victim;[23] and a man's forced sexual intercourse with his wife is not considered to be rape.[24] The Jordanian legislation differs from Egyptian law in such matters, although the Egyptian Penal Code is the historical source of its Jordanian counterpart. The Egyptian law considers a man's intercourse with a female without her consent to be a rape, making no exception of the husband.[25]

In designating adultery a crime, the Jordanian Penal Code uses the term 'adultress' for the woman[26] but the man is termed the 'accomplice'. When setting penalties, it stresses the punishment of the woman and makes maximum penalty for her two years in prison, to be applied regardless of whether the incident occurred in the marital home or not. The maximum penalty a husband incurs, however, is one year in prison, which may be imposed only when he commits adultery in his marital home.

The law of adultery is applicable not only to his wife, as in Egyptian law for example,[27] but includes in its scope the *mahramat* – close female relatives in a degree of consanguinity to the male that makes marriage to them forbidden under Islamic law. But there is no provision for the inclusion of the male *maharim*, that is, male relatives in a similar relation to the female. Thus only a man's wife may proceed against him, but if, for example, a woman found her husband in bed with a woman other than her mother, she could not raise criminal proceedings against him. In any case, the law decrees joint prosecution of man and woman, so that if proceedings against one of them are dropped, the prosecution of the other also lapses.

The law also holds adultery to be a justification for murder, in, for example, cases where the husband comes upon his wife or one of his female *mahram* relatives engaging in adultery, and as a result kills her.[28] If on the other hand a wife finds her husband or one of her male *mahram* relatives in the same position, and she kills him, she will be given the maximum penalty for murder, which can mean the death sentence.[29]

The essence of the situation is that the law considers the woman as part of the man's property, and protects her as he protects his other possessions.[30] It is interesting to note here an example of honour crimes among Palestinians in Lebanon, as described by Rosemary Sayigh:

> Honour killings still occasionally occur in the camps, but it would be hard to find anyone to defend them as part of the Palestinian cultural heritage. Rather, they are looked at as a symptom of political frustration. When in 1973, after a serious confrontation with the Lebanese regime, there was a spate of five honour killings in Tal-al-Za'ter camp, a deputation of women went to the PLO Chairman, Yasser Arafat, to ask him to stop this kind of crime which had almost died out in the refugee period.[31]

Regarding women's work in this period, the lack of sufficient employment opportunites for the refugees, together with the concentration of most new projects in the East Bank, meant that collective women's work in the Jordanian period was directed towards relief and charity work. Charitable societies were set up, comprised mostly of middle-class women.

This situation was reinforced by the policy pursued by the Jordanian government in adopting Bedouin values to the detriment of Palestinian urban/peasant values, as stated above. Another factor was the extent of political restriction enforced by the Jordanian regime; for most of the time between 1948 and 1967, Jordan was subject to the provisions of Emergency Regulations,[32] by virtue of which the government curtailed basic freedoms.[33] The laws on charitable societies also placed many restrictions on women's societies.

The first Jordanian law on charitable societies was promulgated in 1956. It provided for strict supervision of the activities of the societies, calling, for example, for the dissolution of the society either in the absence of appointed supervisors at meetings or if search of sites or records was refused. This position was maintained and strengthened in the other laws on charitable societies that followed. The 1956 Law had allowed societies to object before the High Court of Justice if their applications for registration were refused, but the Law of 1966 abrogated this right.

When women did call for discussion on certain women's issues and problems, they found themselves facing difficulties not only from the traditionalists, but also from the ruling authorities. When some members of the Arab Women's Federation in Nablus invited female professionals, including a poet, a doctor, and an educational expert to discuss the status of women, they not only had to convince the traditionalists of the significance of the conference, but also to obtain permission for it from the Administrative Governor; and in order for permission to be granted the Federation had to promise not to discuss 'political' topics.[34]

Despite the political and social changes that have taken place in the West Bank since 1967, the legal provisions governing the position of women have remained little changed since the Jordanian period.

Women after the 1967 War

On 5 June 1967, the June War broke out, and when it ended the remainder of Palestine – the West Bank and Gaza Strip – along with the Syrian Golan Heights and the Egyptian Sinai Desert were occupied by Israel.

Military Proclamation No. 2, issued by the Israeli Army Command in the West Bank, on 7 June 1967, transferred all the legislative, executive and administrative powers previously held by the Jordanian government to the General Military Commander for the West Bank region. All the laws in force at the time of occupation were to remain unchanged, unless modified by other provisions from the Israeli Military Commander.

International law has two provisions that may permit the occupying authority to change previously existing local laws: either that a change is necessary for the security of the occupying power, or in the interest of the local inhabitants. Since the 1967 occupation, however, the Israeli authorities have modified many of the existing Jordanian laws in such a way as to accord with their own goals – the Judaization of the Occupied Territories and the prevention of the establishment of a Palestinian state for example. The changes they have made contravene the texts of international agreements and conventions concerning areas under occupation. To date, the Israeli authorities have issued a staggering 1,180 or so Military Orders.[35]

International law requires that the Israeli legislation modify local laws which pertain to vital civil affairs in order to accommodate social development and thus protect the well-being of the persons in the occupied territory. The substantial quantity of military orders issued by the Israeli military authorities, however, do not deal with such laws. Instead the military legislator has not only changed laws to suit Israel's own interests,[36] as we have seen, but left others as they stand with only minimal modifications, as in issuing related military orders to protect his own particular concerns,[37] or in enforcing their strict application, as in the case of the Jordanian laws pertaining to charitable and co-operative societies.[38] With two exceptions the legal texts relating to the status of women have remained as they were in the Jordanian period.

The first exception is the law of personal status. As noted above, personal status has been within the jurisdiction of religious courts, whether *shari'a*

(Islamic) or church courts since the beginning of the century. These courts have thus remained entirely outside the powers of the Israeli military government in the West Bank, and in turn the Israelis have made no serious attempt to bring them under their authority. This has resulted in these courts applying modifications introduced into Jordanian law after 1967 on issues that lie within their competence, despite the post-1967 freezing of Jordanian law applied in the West Bank. An example of this is that since 1978 the *shari'a* courts in the West Bank have been practising the new Law of Personal Status for Muslims issued the same year in Jordan, although officially it is not applied in the West Bank.[39]

Perhaps the most important point in the new law is that it gives the wife the right to demand compensation for 'arbitrary' divorce, and enables her to seek a maximum compensation equivalent to one year's maintenance. This is extremely significant, as it goes against classical Islamic law which holds *talaq* (divorce) to be the unilateral right of the husband, who may enforce it whenever he wishes, without having to show reason or justification. Despite the importance of this provision, however, it should be noted that the *talaq* itself stands and is not voided, as are the *talaq* of the madman and the drunkard.[40]

There are, however, other provisions that should be reconsidered, such as the tolerance of polygamy, which, for example, has been banned by Tunisia and restricted by Iraqi and Syrian law, and also out-of-court *talaq*, which is legal in Jordan, but which again has been rectified in the legislation of other Arab countries.

The second exception is something that the Israelis usually point to as proof of their concern for the development of the legal status of Palestinian women. Military Order 627 of 1976 gives women voting and candidacy rights in municipal posts. This Order abrogated the provisions in the Jordanian Law of Municipalities that confined such rights to males.[41] I would, however, suggest that the main motive of the Israelis in giving women the vote at that time was not, as they claim, concern on their part to improve women's legal status. That this claim is untenable may be seen from the fact that they have changed no other single provision whatsoever relating to women's legal status. Rather, the move was made for purely political reasons related to the interest of Israeli policy in the West Bank.

In 1976, at the time of new municipal elections in the West Bank, Israel was extremely worried that the results would favour the Palestine Liberation Organisation (PLO). Because the PLO supporters consisted mainly of the youth, many traditional leaders, who had dubious qualifications to say the least, were pushed by the Israelis into entering the election campaign. It may well be that the Israelis gave women the right to vote at that particular time in order to boost the position of these leaders, on the assumption that women were in general not interested in political issues, and would probably follow family ties in casting their vote. At that time, as we have noted, the women's movement was still more or less confined to charitable societies comprised mainly of middle-class women.

The 1976 elections, however, once again brought victory for PLO supporters in the West Bank, thus leading to the freezing of the 1980 elections. In March 1982 the occupying authorities dissolved most of the municipal councils in the West Bank and appointed new committees in their place, mostly headed by Israeli officers. Municipal elections in the West Bank are still frozen after more than seven years. The Israelis refuse to allow new elections to be held, fearing that the PLO supporters would again win. (In my opinion, however, there are many other reasons, but for questions of space these cannot be discussed here.) Thus, during the occupation, women have exercised their right to vote only once, and when the results of the election were contrary to the expectations of the occupying authorities, municipal elections were banned completely.

The Israeli authorities have also obstructed societies and unions by refusing to register them, and have restricted their work by applying provisions from Jordanian law, some of which were mentioned above. Despite these restrictions there is today a wide, strong, and popular women's movement which holds that social liberation must come side by side with political liberation, and which exerts every possible effort towards the realization of these goals.

Since the beginning of the occupation, Israeli policies in the Occupied Territories have aimed to Judaize the land, obliterate the Palestinian identity, and prevent the establishment of an independent Palestinian state. These policies have obliged the West Bank women's charitable societies to change the direction they pursued under the Jordanian regime. Now women's movement activities focus on steadfastness in the land, preservation of Palestinian cultural heritage, and support of the inhabitants of the occupied land in the burdens of daily life. Perhaps the best example here is the role of the *In'ash al-Usra* society of al-Bireh.

The *In'ash al-Usra* society was founded in 1965. At the outbreak of the 1967 war it began to provide support for the families of martyrs as well as shelter and aid for refugees. It quickly found, however, that this role had to be expanded to undertake small-scale income-generating projects. The Society established a sewing workshop for women and then oversaw a project for processing and wrapping foodstuffs. Neither of these were successful, however, and the Society began to change its focus. Conscious of a need to preserve the Palestinian heritage, it undertook a project based on embroidering and knitting traditional Palestinian clothes. It then set up literacy classes, and programmes for training young women in secretarial work and beauty culture.

In 1976 a number of young, progressive Palestinian women met together to examine and evaluate women's activities in the West Bank. They found them to be almost entirely limited to the largely charitable, middle-class oriented groups holding traditional views of women and helping them to cope with their life only in a role supportive to men; the training they offered was confined to those types of work traditionally considered 'suitable' for women.

This group of progressive young women, believing that a women's movement linking social to national liberation and including women of all classes was needed, began to work on the formation of women's committees. At present, there are four women's committees in the West Bank. Their activities are based around villages and camps, and the representation and participation of the village and camp women themselves in the work, decision-making and general policy is built into the committees' structures.

The various projects have so far proceeded on the basis of helping women to get out of the home, broadening their perceptions of women's rights and freedom, and helping them to overcome their daily problems in order to free them for productive (paid?) work. Child-care centres and kindergartens have been opened in many places, and clinics have been established to help solve the health problems in the villages. Literacy classes have also been set up in the villages in the belief that illiteracy is a basic obstacle to women's participation in productive work. The committees have also started various projects to help women become qualified in non-traditional fields. They have prepared studies concerning women's status and issued publications describing their ideas and strategies and urging working women to join unions. They have campaigned for equal pay for women, and for legal rights such as maternity leave. They have also succeeded in having International Women's Day recognized as a paid holiday in a considerable number of West Bank institutions.

There is discussion among the various women's committees as to whether priority should be given first to political liberation and then to social liberation, or whether the two issues should proceed together. The feelings on this are illustrated by the answer given by a representative of the Women's Work Committee[42] when she was asked about men's role in women's liberation in the Occupied Territories and women's role in the liberation of men:

> Man will not share in the liberation process of woman; it is woman alone who undertakes this task, and who works for her own liberation both from the employer and sexually from the man. Man has a supporting role, but the basic role is woman's. The liberation of woman and of man is linked to the process of liberation on both social and national levels; woman and man are both subjected to oppression in both the Palestinian and the wider pan-Arab sphere. With regard to the role of women in the liberation of man, woman does not oppress man so she should not work for his liberation; woman must achieve her own demands to be equal with man, taking maternity and child leave etc; woman must fight double the struggle of man, and after liberation woman's role will be in social struggle; and this, we believe, is a struggle of profound tenacity.

The women's committees co-ordinate their activities with other Palestinian institutions, making women's work an active and influential factor in Palestinian society, and one that greatly contributes towards influencing the course of events in the West Bank.

Notes

1. The provisions of the *Majalla* still apply in the West Bank.

2. This was the case throughout the Ottoman period, and was confirmed in Articles 51 and 52 of the 1922 Palestine Order-in-Council (text in Robert Harry Dritton, 'Law of Palestine', p. 3303).

3. Miryam Mar'i paper entitled 'Women's Movements in Palestine in the period before the Disaster', presented to the First Conference of Palestinian Thought, held in Nazareth 10–12 May 1985 (Arabic text).

4. Examples of such women are Mughannam Wasmi Tubi, Wahida al-Khalidi and Zulaykha al-Shahabi etc.

5. Ghazi al-Khalili, *Palestinian Woman and the Revolution*, Acre (Dar al-Aswar publications) p. 80 (Arabic text).

6. 'Isa al-Safari, *Palestine between the Mandate and Zionism*, Part One, p. 176 (Arabic text).

7. Miryam Mar'i, op cit.

8. Ibid.

9. Rosemary Sayigh, *Palestinians: From Peasants to Revolutionaries*, London, Zed Press, 1979, pp. 22–3.

10. Ibid., p. 16.

11. The Historical Resolution to Unify the Two Banks: text on p. 4 of the Body of Laws and Regulations Issued and Valid in the Hashemite Kingdom of Jordan until 1956 (Arabic text).

12. Suhair Salati al-Tell, *Prefaces to the Women's Question and to the Women's Movement in Jordan*, Beirut, first edition 1985, p. 18 (Arabic text).

13. Ibid., p. 21.

14. Ibid., pp. 26, 29.

15. This view is also supported by the Jordanian researcher Suhair al-Tell, op cit., p. 108.

16. Art. 30 of the Jordanian Constitution, published in No. 1093 of the Official Gazette on 8/1/52.

17. Ibid.

18. Art. 2 of the Temporary Law of Election for the Jordanian Council of Deputies, Law No. 24 of 1964, defines 'a Jordanian' for the purposes of this law as being 'every male person holding Jordanian nationality'. This provision was amended in Jordan in 1975 to include women, but the amendment does not apply to the West Bank.

19. Jordanian Constitution, Art. 6.

20. Jordanian Law of Family Rights, Law No. 29 of 1952.

21. Lynn Welchman, 'Law in the West Bank: Historical Development since the Ottoman period', unpublished dissertation, London 1985, p. 66.

22. Cassation 56/82: the *Jordanian Bar Association Gazette*, 1982, p. 890.

23. Art. 308 of Jordanian Penal Code, Law No. 16 of 1960, published p. 374 of the Official Gazette No. 8714 on 1/5/60.

24. Jordanian Penal Code, Art. 392.

25. Art. 267 of the Egyptian Penal Code, Law No. 58 of 1937 published in *al-waqa'i' al-misriyya* No. 71 of 5/8/37. This has been amended several times and is still valid in Egypt.

26. Jordanian Penal Code, Art. 383.

27. Ibid., Art. 340.

28. Egyptian Penal Code, Arts. 273–7.

29. Jordanian Penal Code, Arts. 326 and 328.

30. The law absolves from penalty the man who kills while legitimately defending his own or another's person, his or another's honour or his or another's property; Art. 341 Jordanian Penal Code.

31. Rosemary Sayigh, op. cit., p. 25.

32. This continues to be the case.

33. See for example Defence Regulation No. 5 of 1954 pertaining to Public Assemblies, and Defence Regulation No. 5 of 1952, which bans radio owners in public places from broadcasting certain programmes. There are many other examples.

34. Raymonda Tawil, *My Home, My Prison*, London, Zed Press, 1983 pp. 17, 73.

35. For more on Israeli policy towards the Occupied Territories and its relation to international law, see for example Raja Shehadeh, 'Occupier's Law – Israel and the West Bank', Washington (Institute for Palestine Studies) 1985.

36. As happened when the Israeli military legislator issued Military Order 854 by virtue of which restrictions were imposed on academic freedom. See further: Atallah Kuttab, 'An Analytical Study of Military Order 854 and other Orders relating to Educational Institutions', Law in the Service of Man publication, Ramallah, West Bank 1981.

37. As happened, for example, in the Jordanian Penal Code when Military Order 378 was issued, called 'Order Relating to Security Regulations', which banned many activities besides those forbidden by the Penal Code and established military courts to deal with offenders. For the text of the order, see the present author's 'Collection of Military Orders relating to Military Courts and Prisons as amended until 1/7/82', Ramallah (LSM publication) 1982.

38. For additional information see Raja Shehadeh, op cit.

39. Lynn Welchman, op. cit., p. 93.

40. See further Raja Shehadeh and Jonathan Kuttab, 'The West Bank and the Rule of Law', ICJ Publications, 1980, pp. 21–2.

41. See for example Ethia Simha, 'The Status of Arab Women in Judea, Samaria and the Gaza Strip', unpublished report, Jerusalem, July 1984.

42. The Women's Work Committee was the first to be established and is the strongest in terms of activity and membership.

8. Women and Health in the Arab World

May Haddad

The present state of health

A healthy human being is one who controls his/her circumstances. By that I mean the individual who understands and controls all the factors that influence his/her life, be they economic, social, political, cultural or health factors. Health, however, does not receive due attention in the Arab region despite the fact that our health profoundly affects our performance. The hopes created by medical progress at the beginning of the 20th century have, for the most part, been frustrated, as the following figures reveal: 60% of the population of developing countries receive no medical care; 50% of the population of developing countries have no clean water; 20% of the population of developing countries suffer from severe malnutrition. Thus the gap between the developing and developed countries is progressively increasing.

In Africa, one in seven infants die before the age of one year, in Asia one in ten, as against one in 40 in the industrial countries. Maternal mortality is 100–200 times higher in the developing countries than in the developed industrial world. In many regions this is largely due to illegal abortions. Such statistics point to the need for radical changes in global policies in favour of the affected countries if the target determined by the World Health Organization and 'theoretically' adopted by most countries of 'Health to All by the Year 2000' is to become a reality. A change in global policies means in the first place a limitation of armaments (industrial countries spend $510 billion annually on armaments, an amount sufficient to feed a population 25 times the size of the world population today). Maldistribution of resources, particularly between rural and urban areas in developing countries should be rectified. (Only 20% of resources is spent on rural areas which accommodate 80% of the population.)

In addition to the discrimination between developed and developing countries, rural and urban areas, sex discrimination is revealed by the following figures: women's labour accounts for two-thirds of total labour hours; women earn less than 10% of world income and own less than one hundredth of total property. Women are clearly the victims of very unhealthy circumstances.

While a woman should, theoretically, be the focus of all health efforts since she is the reproducer, the primary carer for child health and is in charge of all feeding matters, still her own health is constantly deteriorating. Even in the developed countries, women today suffer from a number of psychological problems precipitated by modern lifestyles.

Factors affecting women's health

The social status of women
In Arab society, women work hard at domestic chores (cooking, cleaning, washing, and so on) performed in the home as well as other chores they undertake outside the home (fetching water, farming, raising cattle, among others).

Will the role of Palestinian women regress once Palestinians are able to exercise their right to self-determination? This is a difficult question, but I can see many indications that Palestinian women will indeed be able to maintain their current gains if national state rule is established. For this to occur, however, national state rule must be established on the principle of the rule of law and human rights, must set women's rights and freedoms among its priorities, and must openly consider the importance of this struggle in the development of a Palestinian society based on equality and justice.

Particularly in the rural areas, women's work can be very exhausting and is neither materially nor morally appreciated, which can be frustrating. Women are also expected to maintain certain attitudes towards marriage, virginity and fertility, and to conform to the dominant customs and traditions, often so stressful that psychological distress results.

Women, again particularly in the rural areas, are more vulnerable to malnutrition and its related diseases precipitated by repeated childbirth and inadequate diets. In certain societies, food is served first to men, then to children, and the women must make do with the leftovers. Women are subjected to such harmful practices as circumcision, which have negative effects on their health. These problems are aggravated by the fact that no serious efforts are taken to tackle these issues from a woman's perspective, but always and only by men on her behalf.

Health policies
In Arab countries, health services receive the least allocations of national budgets and are primarily directed to the construction of hospitals in cities with sophisticated technology along Western models. Such edifices cater to the privileged élite. (A study conducted in North Yemen showed that all hospitals built in three of the major cities serve no more than 7% of the population.) Allocations to such health-conducive activities as clean water supply networks, nutrition, sewerage systems, and so on, are either very scarce or barely existent.

Male domination of the medical sector
Men have come to dominate the sphere of curative medicine and to oust women

from competition in this field. The male gynaecologist, for example, has declared the illegitimacy of the practice of midwifery and undermined the value and effectiveness of herbs and traditional diets which women had developed and have passed on from generation to generation.

Male doctors seem to go about their practice apparently unaccountable to any higher authority. There has been no attempt to investigate the reasons for the increasing rates of Caesarian sections, hysterectomies, suction deliveries and artificial induction of labour by way of Oxytocin. In the field of medicine men are the symbols of power, in keeping with the pattern of power distribution in the society, while women are allocated the role of the ignorant, the sick and the helpless.

The role of pharmaceutical companies
Pharmaceutical companies are inundating the Arab markets with medicines dispensed off the counter with, in most cases, no control. The result is an excessive use of medicines perpetuated by both the doctor and the patient; the doctor prescribes the medicines because the patient wishes to take them. In addition, the same formula may exist under a number of brand names and sold at different prices. According to one World Health Organization (WHO) survey, there are 300,000 brand names on the market of which only 200 are essential. Medicines are a deadly weapon and are responsible for many of our modern diseases, but this fact is concealed by those with vested interests. Arab countries, as well as other developing countries, are used as dumping grounds for drugs which are either unmarketable or which are prohibited on medical grounds in the West. Depo-provera, an injectable contraceptive drug, is available on our markets but prohibited in the USA. The wide range of medicines in this category include not only contraceptives, but also vitamins, stimulants of no effect and antibiotics which could even have a deadly effect. Women are the main consumers of these 'health aids'.

Pharmaceutical companies may also market insecticides, other chemicals or even cosmetic products which could damage health. To this we should add the inundation of our markets with tinned foods and milk products – especially baby formulae which are accompanied by misleading advertising campaigns. The harmful effects of these milk formulae is now well recognized.

Means of empowering women through their health

By the beginning of the 1970s, the adequacy of the curative system and the effectiveness of the Western model and its adoption by developing countries were seriously questioned. In 1987, the challenge ultimately led to the declaration of a moratorium by United Nations International Children's Emergency Fund (UNICEF), WHO and government representatives. The meeting adopted an instrument for primary health care which was defined as: 'basic health care which relies on means and technologies that are practical, scientifically sound, socially acceptable and affordable by the majority of individuals and families in the community who could be fully involved, at a cost which the community or country could supply stage by stage in its development, in a spirit of self dependence and free will.'

Primary health care should comprise at least the following services:

- raising community awareness of prevailing health problems and means of controlling them;
- provision of food and the propagation of adequate diets;
- supply of clean water;
- maternity and child care and family planning;
- immunization;
- prevention and control of endemic diseases;
- treatment of common diseases and injuries;
- provision of essential drugs.

Discussion of primary health care resulted in the establishment of a new cadre of health workers, who are envisaged as persons living in the community and aware of its problems. In this respect, there was a strong move to involve women in this cadre after giving them adequate training. There was also a call to draw on local resources and as far as possible to integrate traditional practitioners who, in some areas, are the only persons involved in therapy, for example bone setters, traditional midwives, *zar sheikhas* (exorcizers of evil spirits), and so on; women often play a leading role in such professions.

Our Arab culture is rich in therapeutic prescriptions based on herbs. Camomile, hibiscus flowers, fenugreek, rice water, mint, anise, and many other herbs are noted for their medicinal properties.

In order to upgrade primary health care, a new approach to education and training based on an understanding of the problems of the community should be adopted. This will ensure that relevant skills are acquired which, as far as possible, take into consideration positive prevailing customs and practices.

In many Arab countries, there is now a movement involving both men and women endeavouring to demystify medicine and other fields of the health services. They promote activities that will empower women's health awareness and exchange health information.

In conclusion, I would like to remind you of the recommendations related to health issued by the Conference on Women, in Nairobi in July 1985.

- Women's leading role in safeguarding the health of the family within the home and outside it should be recognized. (para. 148)
- Women have the right to control their fertility, and it is the duty of governments and local organizations to propagate family planning practices for both men and women, and to encourage men to shoulder their responsibilities regarding the health of their families. Governments should ensure that contraceptives distributed are safe and effective. (paras. 150, 156, 157, 159, 121, 125)
- Basic health services should be supported, more efforts should be made to eradicate endemic diseases, to limit the risks to women's health and to

encourage women to strive for realizing the objective of 'Health to All by the Year 2000'. (paras. 148, 155)
- Governments should seek to prohibit the marketing of useless and harmful drugs. (para. 153)
- Efforts should be made to enhance the participation of women in higher medical specialization, key administrative positions in health organizations and to encourage a larger involvement of women in training, and their representation on health committees at both community and national levels. Employment terms for women health workers should be improved at all levels. (para. 149)
- Midwives and women involved in healing practices should be effectively integrated into national health schemes. (para. 149)
- Governments should consult with women and solicit their help in the planning and implementation of water projects for hygienic purposes. (paras. 151, 152)
- Governments should combat health hazards at work sites for both male and female workers, particularly hazards affecting the female reproductive system. (paras. 162, 194)
- Governments should raise awareness regarding the nutritional needs of women, and support women's right to a three months' leave before delivery and leave during the nursing period. Governments should combat diseases of malnutrition such as anaemia which affect women at different ages and should support and develop local food products used during weaning, by supporting relevant projects for such purposes. (para. 154)

Bibliography

1. Bowker/Unipub/Unesco Bibliographic Studies on the Status of Women, 1st edition 1983.

2. Cottingham, J. 'Health and Development', *Women in Development: a resource guide for organizations and action. ISIS* 1984.

3. Humphrey Institute of Public Affairs, *Forward Looking Strategies for the Advancement of Women to the Year 2000*. University of Minnesota 1986.

4. Illich, Ivan, *Medical Nemesis*.

5. JUNIC/NGO Sub-group on Women and Development. Women, Health & Development, Geneva, 1981.

6. Leeson, J. & Judith Gray, *Women & Medicine*, Tavistock Publications UK, 1987.

7. UNESCO, *Women in the Arab World*, Social Science Research, UNESCO, 84.

9. Women and Health in Sudan

Nahid Toubia

Women, as an integral part of society, are affected by those economic factors that have an impact on the health of society as a whole. Adequate food supplies and effective clinical health services on the one hand, and raising health awareness as well as the provision of preventive health measures on the other, are factors that determine the level of health of a society in general.

Certain health problems, however, aggravate women's physical and psychological burden, adding to the already heavy load of a complex social heritage. Such problems ensue from the nature of the socio-cultural structure in each society, generating a peculiar set of individual and collective rituals and traditions. Such ritual and tradition have a greater impact on women than on men as the former are bearers of family honour, and are bartered for a price at marriage, hence they should appear before the eyes of society in the most beautiful and perfect state.

The way a woman relates to her body and the psychological reflection of this image on her are, in any society, directly related to both the status of women in that society and the reflected ideal of femininity imposed upon them. Such a conditioning process evidently bears both physically and psychologically on women. True, some common features and preliminary indicators regarding the status of women seem to be universal today, yet each community has its unique socio-economic structure affecting women in various ways, which may at times seem parallel but may vary infinitely in details. In Western societies for example, there are basic social patterns that govern the relations between a man and a woman, between two women and of the woman with herself. The whole social structure is built around the nuclear family unit, with power exercised from within that family unit with no external influence from close or distant relatives. Then comes the economic factor. The individual's income is related to the labour market, and its direct financial transactions. The families of the individuals concerned are not depended upon to provide direct or indirect financial or other forms of support, consequently there are no overt or subtle pressures to pay back such family favours. Services are institutionalized in industrialized societies. State as well as private institutions cater to the individual's needs in the fields of education, employment, social and health insurance, and so on; an individual is not usually compelled to turn to her/his family support network for the fulfilment of such needs. S/he is a productive unit capable of selling her/his labour to buy the quality of life s/he chooses.

Psychologically, an individual in Western society is encouraged to develop her/his unique personality. Individuality could be a means of freeing creativity and innovation, but could equally lead to self-centred, self-protective behaviour even to the extent of alienation – the loss of any sense of belonging. This by no means denies that such societies have their own rituals and social traditions nor that there is a social majority that exerts pressures of conformity on the individual's choice, but this psychological factor is much weaker in Western than in Middle Eastern societies, because the final arbitration between individual and collective interests in the West is secular law.

Thus, industrialized societies have converted the individual into a consumer of goods and services offered by capital to generate the jobs the consumers need in order to survive and to continue consuming. At this point we should consider a basic difference between Western and Middle Eastern societies on matters concerning women. To pursue their lives, both physically and socially, women in contemporary Western societies have the choice to marry or to remain single. They may support themselves by selling their labour, and there is a social space for them as single women. In Middle Eastern societies the overwhelming majority of women (85% in some countries) are illiterate, and work opportunities outside the home are scarce. Women's work is restricted to the home, the family business or land. Survival outside the family is physically impossible. This vital and practical reality should not be overlooked when we assess Arab women's decision-making powers. In cases where a woman owns some property or income generated by inheritance there is still no 'social space' to accommodate her if she remains unmarried. Hence, Arab women in general, and Sudanese women in particular, can survive only within the institutions of marriage and the family – they have no other choice.

Meantime, however, I shall here look more closely at those health problems of women in Western society created by the socio-economic structure already mentioned. In such highly consumerist societies selling the products remains the prime and ultimate goal of the economic powers controlling the society, that is 'capital'. It activates the longstanding social norms of heterosexuality and women's seductive role within it. The media is then mobilized as an increasingly more effective way of imposing certain social attitudes and promoting them as the norm to further serve its own purposes. In fact, despite the apparent progress made by women in the West, the media there still promotes the outdated ideas of woman as a sex object, on the one hand the seductress, and on the other the passive recipient of male sexual drive. Within these boundaries women are made to see themselves as objects of pleasure and are used as advertising material valued only for their physical appearance with its implicit and explicit appeal for sex.

Through these tactics capital endeavours – with a fair degree of success – to sell almost anything to women: cosmetics, fashion clothes, perfume, diet food, sports clothes and much more. By these means women are exhorted to strive constantly to achieve that media model of perfection which is impossible, because it is an illusion and its components are constantly changing according to 'fashion'. These tactics are intended to permanently chain women to the market and the never-ending cycle of consumption. Also through women's bodies and sexual messages men are encouraged to consume what they do and do not need, from after-shave to computers, to tractors, posing a constant challenge to their manliness (another word for virility) with the implicit promise that maybe one day they will be rewarded with all the promises of a sexy woman. Many women in Western societies are victims of a dependence on and addiction to tranquillizers, sleeping tablets and alcohol as a result of pressures on them because of jobs outside the home or, because as housewives, they have to cope with the disillusion and the sense of worthlessness experienced, particularly after menopause when children leave the home and the women's positive role in life seems to have ended. One of the potentially very serious diseases that has recently become widespread in the West is anorexia nervosa, an illness that results from excessive dieting and takes the form of an obsessive preoccupation with slimness, leading eventually to a semi-permanent loss of appetite. The motive is evidently a keen desire to reach the model of slimness publicized by the media. This disease can eventually lead to severe and incapacitating malnutrition and the progressive deterioration in health may become irreversible and ultimately cause death; it is, of course, almost exclusively a disease of women.

Arab societies have many common features: they share the same predominant religion and language, and the basic structural unit of the society, that is, the extended family. Women's lives are, therefore, in many respects similar. Urban lifestyles have checked the propagation of the pattern of one extended family sharing one household, but the economic and psychological relations of the extended family still prevail. They still constitute the mainstay of the relation between the individual and the group and even between separate individuals. The tribe, the class, the *housh* (extended family residence) and the big family remain the geographical, psychological and economic unit in most rural areas.

In Arab society individuals are taught that the group takes precedence, and the importance of belonging to the majority and rejecting individuality is stressed. This psycho-social concept leads to a close and coherent society that provides the individual with a strong sense of protection and security; a friendly atmosphere of familiarity, affection and harmony. It can, however, also lead to fear of change or of developing an individual opinion, and thus inhibit and restrict a person's ability to choose, question and create.

To make a comparison or to judge between Western and Middle Eastern social systems, is too extensive an undertaking to be contained within the limits of this chapter, but I would like to focus on the psycho-social concepts that shape Arab societies in general and Sudanese society in particular, with the aim of finding remedies to our illnesses. If we are genuinely and seriously concerned with change for the better and to achieve our goals of cultural excellence we must analyse our societies objectively in a process of open self-criticism. Only with a scientifically guided, compassionate appraisal of our present situation can we confront our mistakes with the courage and determination of a people confident of themselves, their culture and their heritage. We should be able to retain the most valuable qualities in our societies – self-denial and group coherence – without stifling the individual's potential for creativity and choice.

Some health problems of Sudanese women

I have chosen the model of Sudanese women partly because I am myself a Sudanese woman and am concerned about women's health. The only means to achieve progress in this area are, as I have already stated, through rigorous self-criticism while searching for and opening up the dark crevices of our societies and often those of our own minds.

Some of the practices cited below may at first glance seem inhuman or horrifying, but in essence they differ little from many harmful practices involving women in other societies, even though these may be more subtle in their effect because of social and cultural guise.

Female circumcision

Over the last decade the issue of female circumcision has received wide exposure by Western media and international organizations as well as national bodies. The West has acted as though they have suddenly discovered a dangerous epidemic which they then sensationalized in international women's forums creating a backlash of over-sensitivity in the concerned communities. They have portrayed it as irrefutable evidence of the barbarism and vulgarity of underdeveloped countries, a point of view they have always promoted. It became a conclusive validation to the view of the primitiveness of Arabs, Muslims and Africans all in one blow.[1]

Nevertheless, female circumcision is an important and serious problem that both Arab and African women must approach and tackle. Its serious consequences arise from its deep influence on women both physically and psychologically and from the fact that it has withstood all aspects of change in the societies where it is prevalent. Pharonic circumcision or infibulation is still practised on over 85% of all Sudanese women with the exception of women of the three southern regions, the remote areas of Western Sudan and the Nuba mountains.[2] In fact, the most recent statistics revealed that 98% of females in the northern regions are circumcised, regardless of their level of education (or rather the level of the parents' education) social class or degree of health awareness,[3] including the daughters of doctors, university professors, educationalists, and social workers, for example.

In the majority of cases pharonic circumcision (excision of the clitoris, labia minora and labia majora with stitching of the raw edges over the urethral meatus) or intermediate circumcision (excision of labia minora and clitoris with stitching) are performed. Admittedly there are some indications that over the last three years there is a shift towards excision of clitoris only (sunna circumcision). The social implications of the continuity of the practice and its sexual and psychological effects are, however, still the same, regardless of the degree of surgical cutting. The objective is, therefore, that a girl must have a *tihara* (purification) and is socially and psychologically unacceptable in an uncircumcised *ghalaja* state; one of the most important reasons for circumcising a girl is to ensure that she will not lose her chance to marry; as I have already explained this would mean that she loses her chance for a respectable life. Loss of a woman's genitalia is not, therefore, too high a price to pay in order to secure her chances in life through marriage. This is the social significance of female circumcision and its real value. To argue against this practice on the grounds of its physical damage and to attempt to eradicate it through health awareness and education are futile. It is essentially a social phenomenon reflecting the position of women and not a medical problem.

Throughout their recent history, Sudanese women have been circumcised, and they know of no other state to be. They cannot therefore develop their conscience from within to demand their right to keep their genitals intact. For a Sudanese woman to be without external genitals is the normal state of female anatomy and all her accumulated experience on sexuality and her normal body responses have been inherited from generations of circumcised women. How can she possibly penetrate the thick walls of accumulated misconceptions amongst women and overcome the conspiracy of silence that society has woven over the issue?

Let us also question how a Sudanese mother (herself circumcised at the age of 4–8 years) can choose not to circumcise her daughter? She will alienate her from her peer group and from the other women in the family, for they are all circumcised. Even if the parents are convinced that they do not want to mutilate their daughter, how can they possibly antagonize the grandmothers, the aunts and the whole family? It is necessary to think of ways to change the beliefs of the extended family and the group, and not restrict our arguments to individualistic conviction for that is too weak against group pressure. The individual in our societies cannot stand alone against the pressures exerted by the group. Our efforts must be geared towards finding a language that will communicate to society as a whole. We have to convince the group that the benefits of this action (in this case stopping circumcision) will be for the society as a whole and not only the individual. This does not, of course, preclude our appeal to the vanguard of intellectuals who can lead this process of change. It is most essential that we find satisfactory answers to the questions a woman will face when she is debating a stand against the practice. She may ask herself: How can I possibly choose a course of action different from my mother's, my aunts' and my friends'? How can I live if I break away from established tradition and choose a path of newly acquired knowledge and unfamiliar practices? How can I possibly risk the only chance for a life for my daughter (marriage) by not circumcising her?

These are a few among many questions that must be satisfactorily answered if we really want to eradicate the practice.

The use of henna

Dyeing the hands and feet with henna is one of the distinguishing practices of some communities. This intricate art reflects women's creative expressions, and may be considered as an interesting variation in the spectrum of methods of beautifying the body that characterize cultural groups, and that enriches the human life with the exciting variations of creative cosmetics. Henna designing in itself, therefore, cannot be objectionable; on the contrary, the lack of such creative outlets may be a cause of concern as life would become dull and monotonous and we would all look the same. For Sudanese women, however, henna dyeing no longer carries the aesthetic values only but has become a practice binding on all women in their first year of marriage and on every public occasion thereafter, particularly for religious festivities, weddings and even for paying condolences and when receiving well wishers after giving birth. This obligation is the negative side of the practice.

The standards by which the beauty of the henna patterning is measured dictates that the smaller and more complex, intricate and dark the design the better. To attain the desired effect the application must be slow, and the henna left on the hands and feet for hours or even days and applied several times. Natural henna is light in colour and works slowly, and its use means the woman's activities must be restricted and even halted for the whole time it takes to set. This may have been possible in the old, leisurely days when life made fewer demands on women and they were living within the extended family and could receive the physical support that offered. Today, the pace of life is much faster and there are greater demands on the woman who, alone, is responsible for the nuclear family home. A woman cannot afford to be effectively paralysed for hours or days each time an occasion arises; she may be holding a job on top of her household duties. Still the practice is a must and women had to find new ways to attain the same result. A new, black, stone dye (usually used in the formulae of manufactured hair dyes) was called upon. The 'dye', as it is usually called, is a very dangerous chemical and is classified by doctors, chemists and the police research laboratory as a deadly poison. A teaspoonful taken by mouth causes death in a few hours. The more dangerous route is the slow absorption through cracks and abrasions on hands and feet painted with the henna/dye mixture or through the mouth when eating with the hands and feeding the children with fingers. The toxin is then taken in repeatedly small doses resulting in no acute symptoms but passing unnoticed until the woman (or child) suffers renal failure from chronic toxicity.

A few years ago, the Ministry of Health of Sudan collaborated with the Ministry of the Interior and launched an intensive campaign to expose the dangerous effects of the dye, but with no significant effects. The social pressures on women to conform is far greater than the individual ability for reasoning or personal will, regardless of their levels of education. In fact, my experience amongst friends and colleagues is that the highly educated women with responsible, demanding jobs are those who more often use the dye as they have no time for natural henna. They compromise their health in trying to find the balance between the two contradictions of a responsible social position at work and a traditional social expectation of married women who are not threatening to men.

Obesity

To this day obesity is still considered a sign of beauty in a Sudanese woman and amongst Arab women generally. Admittedly, the actual physical sizes are no longer those of pre-Islamic (*johilya*) buffalo dimensions, nevertheless, the desirable weight of a 'sexy' woman is far above the limits acceptable for a healthy body. A contributing factor to excessive weight is the lack of any physical exercise or sporting activity due to social restrictions, particularly after marriage. Preparing big rich, diverse meals and entertaining by providing food are signs of a good, successful wife. Consequently a disproportionate amount of a woman's time is spent in the kitchen, concentrating on food. This overemphasis on food is beyond the healthy needs of a human being and consumes the mental and physical energy needed to take part in other social, cultural and political interests and activities.

Compulsive eating by women is often a symptom of their frustration and depression, and a way of compensating for the absence of personal fulfilment. Eating becomes a habitual substitute for many unexpressed feelings, unrealized dreams and frustrated potentials. The diseases and complications of obesity are well known: hypertension, diabetes, arthritis of the knees are among the commonest.

Psycho-neuroses and depression

Psycho-neuroses and depression are more common amongst women than officially recognized in medical statistics. Very few professionals understand them as a group phenomenon or analyse them as such. Instead they are seen as individual cases and as an expression of maladjustment with society or as a woman's failure to face up to her marital responsibilities as a wife and a mother. They are considered as pathological illnesses divorced from their causes which may be found in the woman's position in the family and in society. Among the manifestations of these conditions are compulsive eating, mentioned above, excessive introversion or extroversion with accompanied endless chattering.

Psychosomatic disease is also widespread among women and this explains the disproportionate numbers of women in doctors' surgeries and clinics. It is often an unconscious cry for help and a plea for a sympathetic ear for their complaints which they are unable to express openly.[4] All these are some of the physical and psychological manifestations of social problems.

How does society perpetuate its values and thus manage to withstand the factors of change such as women's education and increasing cultural, social and political awareness amongst them? Why are modern Sudanese women unable to break away from all these negative social phenomena despite their education and increasing participation in public life?

The need to belong to the group

As I have mentioned earlier, Sudanese society is strongly ethnocentric with a heightened feeling of an individual's need to affiliate to the group. This is compounded by a tribally biased African heritage and an Arab heritage that stresses the importance of strong family lineages. Over the last 20 years, due to harsh economic and political conditions, many families have been dispersed and the individual dislocated from his/her group. This forced separation often strengthens the feelings of belonging and gives rise to the need to jealously guard and protect the manifestations of group identity. Immigrants, for example, may preserve custom and ritual more vigorously, even irrationally, than people in the homeland. In such alienated individuals the need to relate to the roots drives them to hold on even to the brink.

The same process seems to apply to the effects of the social disintegration that has taken place over the last two decades. Not only have people clung to their traditional customs and rituals but have reverted to some previously obsolete practices and reaffirmed them in the face of changes in education, in cultural mixing, and unprecedented extremes of wealth and poverty.

Another very important cause of slow or imperceptible change is the emphasis on compliance and conformity in the indoctrination of children, and the determined rejection of any deviation at all from the prevailing norm. The material and moral losses incurred by loss of identity could not be compensated for by any individual gains, even if these were more progressive. This inherent fear of social isolation, one of the greatest barriers to change in Arab societies, needs to be examined and analysed in order to find out how it should be tackled so as to retain its positive aspects before these are destroyed by the pressures of Western style modernization, leaving selfish individuality to prevail and Arab social identity lost.

The inevitability of marriage for women

In Middle Eastern societies marriage is still a social act in which the involvement of the two individuals concerned is lesser or greater depending on where and when it takes place. In Sudan, marriage is still primarily concerned with a relationship between two families rather than two individuals, and the personal choices of the couple are still of secondary importance. Again, marriage for a woman has an existential absolutism that is inescapable; it does not involve a choice of simple human companionship over solitude, nor is it a response to mutual affection. For a Sudanese woman marriage is a non-choice during which it is difficult to be rational or calm, two prerequisites for taking such a major step as binding oneself to another being. No mental space is left to choose or reject the rituals and customs that accompany this step. Marriage in Sudan is, therefore, still burdened with rituals and practices to be performed by the two families, starting from the initial negotiations and ending in the actual festivities which, to this day, continue for three to seven days among all social groups. Society's insistence upon holding on to its values is manifested by these customs and rituals. The marrying couple neither has the right to object nor the right to choose.

The man is never consulted about whether or not he wants as his bride a circumcised woman, the bride is not asked whether she would like to be saved all the weeks of tedious, exhausting preparations she has to undergo until the day of the wedding. These preparations are mainly aimed at transforming her into a desirable sexual commodity at the expense of extreme physical and psychological stress. Society dictates and individuals must comply as a piece in a chess board moves where it is directed. Women are the most subordinate in the decision-making hierarchy particularly when young and uncrowned by social consent: marriage. Unmarried women remain unrecognized and considered immature regardless of their educational level or degree of personal or intellectual excellence.

How does this tight and complex trap affect the Sudanese woman and formulate her character?

Stages of psychological development of women in Sudan

Stage of alluring

Alluring in early childhood takes two distinct forms. One is the motivation through the rewards gained from acceptance. For example, circumcision is accompanied by a big celebratory feast, with the slaughtering of a sheep, singing, dancing, new clothes, distribution of sweets and receipt of gifts and money. Every girl and boy must dream of the opportunity to become queen or king, the centre of attention and the cause of all this celebration, even for one day.

On the other hand, undergoing such rites of passage means that the child is attaining a new social status in which s/he is considered more mature and deserving of adults' respect. The child must aspire to achieve this status with or without his/her knowledge of the accompanying physical suffering to be endured. This all devolves from the emphasis on the importance of conformity and belonging that is indoctrinated very early in life.

Another motivation, one common to children in all societies, is peer group jealousy which drives the child to imitate his peers in order to overcome any possible sense of alienation or isolation among them. This may drive the child to request such social rites as circumcision or ear-piercing. It is, therefore, imperative that when we tackle these harmful practices, delicate handling of any child whose family decides against performing such rites, is essential.

Stage of intimidation

With the onset of puberty and teenage, physiological, psychological and intellectual changes begin. The question 'why?' takes a deeper meaning and is more frequently present in the youth's mind and s/he starts to question the significance of some of the apparent constants surrounding him/her. All traditional society's forces are mobilized to combat this inquisitive rebellious stage – particularly in the case of women.

Subtle intimidation and not direct threatening is the tactic. Sudanese society is a very sentimental and a gentle, family-oriented society; physical violence is unacceptable, as is direct prohibition. In such a peace-loving atmosphere social pressure must accord with the people's gentle character. The most effective form of intimidation is the fear of upsetting the family; remembering the material and moral importance of family support to the individual, the effectiveness of this fear is understandable. In cases when a young woman persists in her rebellion against social custom and starts taking active steps towards more questioning, or chooses a different path, the mother and other women in the family combine to subdue her. Although it is a male-dominated society the family is organized in such a way (within the household there are separate quarters for men and women) that it is the women's responsibility to put a girl on the acceptable family path. Older women in particular are delegated to be the gatekeepers and internal security bodies in the women's section, and men need only to keep a distant overview of the situation, confident that their wishes and instructions are being observed.

A common form of pressure is the exploitation of the girl's feelings towards her mother and other women in the family. With the almost complete absence of a paternal relationship, a girl becomes totally dependent on the mother emotionally, while the father remains the distant symbol of power and authority devoid of any human intimacy. A mother knows of her daughter's weakness and emotional needs and plays upon them when she needs a disciplinary weapon to set her back on the correct path previously designed for her. All Sudanese women must remember when our mothers got very sick (or allegedly so) or silently sulked so as to put pressure on us to accept a decision made on our behalf. Many people may consider that these methods of intimidation are part of natural family relations, but this complex web of subtle pressure, comprising emotional and material dependence and interests is not always easy to identify.

If a girl cannot clearly see that she is being intimidated she internalizes her rebellion, anger and frustration, and transforms them into guilt and shame for having hurt her loved ones and causing disruption in the family. The outcome is often absolute resignation and submission to all that is dictated to her, and acceptance in shame and repentance.

Stage of adoption

Soon after puberty a young girl reaches the age of marriage with its implications of changes in her social status. Once married, she must forget all her earlier dreams and her rejection of the negative rituals she once thought to rebel against. She has to forego all her individual aspirations and commit herself whole-heartedly to self-denial with the sole purpose of caring for her husband and children, finding herself only in their successes. This process of serial adjustment just pre- and post-marriage entails crossing the threshold of social acceptability – and at the price of numerous psychological and intellectual compromises. A girl must go through a process of 'forced feminization' to gain respect. This raises a persistent question in her subconscious: should she perpetuate her suffering and jeopardize her newly-acquired preferential position, attained through marriage, or utilize the new situation to attain total harmony with those around her. Instincts of self-preservation and the desire for an easy way out almost always win the battle in a society that so fiercely resists social change and condemns individuality. Tactically, it is much more beneficial for the woman to totally adopt prevailing social values or even better be seen to perpetuate them and staunchly resist signs of rebellion in the new generations. Thus the vicious circle repeats itself and the pioneers of change remain few. One of the most important factors that create this new 'adoption' stance is the fear of facing one's own self. When a woman passes through the experience of totally compromising on her own choices and accepts what was dictated and forced upon her, it is very difficult to maintain her self-respect unless she adopts these values as her own and pretends she has always accepted them. This is a self-protecting mechanism against duality and frustration. Endless examples can be cited of women who once refused arranged marriages, insisted on a woman's right to work; rejected the exhaustive prolonged rituals in marriage, and so on, only to completely reverse their stance later and become staunch advocates of the views previously rejected. This reversal often takes the form of a well-argued, intellectually sound conviction that may fool the outsider who could not see what lies behind it. I hope that this analysis may have answered some of the allegations that women are by nature conservative and that it is women who promote negative social practices by inflicting them on their own kind.

Conclusion

While certain harmful concepts and practices that affect women's health are peculiar to Sudan, some are shared with Arab countries. These concepts and practices are closely related to the prevalent moral values, and the distribution of power within the family, which leaves the young unmarried girl at the bottom of the power hierarchy. She must be guarded and moulded by the older women in the family under the detached supervision of the men in the household and the society at large outside it.

It is, therefore, imperative that if change is to be induced we must create the means and methods of circumventing these social structures and not clash with them head on, for they are too powerful and well established. Forceful confrontation with these entrenched structures could either backfire on the women's movement or create irreparable dents and cracks in our social structures. The following points are my contribution towards formulating a tactical approach for change.

1. Approach the group as a whole to neutralize their defences or even win them over to the case for change and avoid as much as possible inciting the individual woman against her class or family. We must avoid alienating individual women or pushing them too far or they will retreat from their initial progressive steps.

2. Promote individuality as a positive value in its free creative sense and work towards incorporating the concept into school curricula. We must set a clear example of how individuality need not be in contradiction to belonging but on the contrary that individual initiative will enrich the group and add to its assets.

3. Discriminate between positive and beautiful customs and harmful and negative ones encouraging the replacement of the latter by the former. This will diffuse the accusations levelled at the women's movement of modernization trends that reject our heritage. Only through compassion can we win people to our point of view.

4. Lastly, change for women will not be brought about by changing just one or a group of social practices. We must emphasize our strong belief that effective change will be brought about within a wider change in the economic and social power structures in the society as a whole. This should guarantee equal opportunities in education and work, plus equal rights and responsibilities inside and outside the home. The balance of social power, particularly within the family and in personal relations, has to be redressed. The sharing of decision-making, planning and executing various activities has to become a reality. This can happen if, while working towards abolishing harmful practices, we link them to the importance of overall change in the basic structures in the society. This socio-economic change is the surest way to radically change women's status and give them the economic and psychological power to realize our dreams.

Notes

1. Seager, J. and Olsen, A., *Women in the World: An International Atlas*, map 4 'Social Surgery', Pan Books, 1986.
2. Toubia, N., 'The Social and Political Implications of Female Circumcision: the case of Sudan' in *Women and the Family in the Middle East*, Elizabeth Fernea (ed.), Texas University Press, 1985.
3. Al Dareer, A., *Woman, Why do you Weep?*, Zed Press, 1983.
4. El Saadawi, N., *Women and Psychoneurosis*, Dar al-Nashr al-Arabi, Beirut, 1978; and Sadig, 'Women and Psychological Disease', in *Ros al-Yussif Magazine*, 28 July 1986, pp. 41–3.

10. The Modern Tunisian Woman between Hysteria and Depression*

Mouinne Chelhi

Introduction

The purpose of this chapter is to present two studies that were recently carried out in Tunisia, one on hysteria and the other on nervous breakdowns amongst Tunisian women. I shall try to interpret the results of these studies in the context of the present evolution of Tunisian society. The aim is not to explain these illnesses in the usual psychiatric terms, by referring to patients' individual biological or physiological characteristics. Instead, the causes of these illnesses will be sought in certain specific social conditions that affect people's lives.

The approach to these two psychiatric illnesses will therefore be firmly set within a sociological and historical framework. The overall idea is that modern Tunisian society imposes upon women (and everyone else) a twofold structuring of social relations, which pulls them in opposite directions. The first structure stems from the traditional agrarian society and tends to subordinate the individual to the social group and permit only the minimum of individual differentiation, while the second stems from modern industrial society – a recent import in Tunisia but which has great impact because it is seen as the direction of the future. This second structure tends to free the individual from the social group and to endow people with a very high degree of individuation. These two contradictory tendencies, acting simultaneously within a person, tend to become split into two incoherent wholes, two levels of psychic life that should be integrated, namely the real, that is, the individual's perception of the social practice of which he or she is a part; and the lived experience, that is the imaginary and the world of desire, as well as the symbolic (the imaginary as mediated through interpersonal interaction and speech). This split between the real and the lived experience is especially serious for a woman, since it is she whom patriarchy most seeks to bind to the law of the group, and she who often makes the greatest strides towards liberating herself from that law.

Our hypothesis is that, when this dichotomy reaches a certain pitch, hysteria and nervous breakdown represent two possible escape routes for a woman. In analysing our sample of hysterical and depressed women, it is hoped to show

* Translated from French by Michael Pallis

that those suffering from these two illnesses can be seen in terms of a scale of relative maturity and immaturity. The hysteric is an immature woman who allows herself to become alienated within a masculine game and who, temporarily at least, loses any means of asserting her identity and desires as a woman. Her strategy is essentially to approach the real through a masculine symbolic, denying her own feminine imagination (her desire). The depressive woman, on the other hand, is an adult who has fulfilled her identity and her desire as a woman, but who is either not recognized or is actually rejected by her social environment because of it. Resistance to any treatment of the illness, which becomes a permanent feature, shows the obstinate attachment of both the woman and of her social milieu to their respective stances of affirmation and rejection.

Hysteria

The study presented here was carried out by the psychiatric service of the Monastir hospital, led by Dr Sleciri. He was kind enough to make the raw data available to me and a group of my Second Year students from the Faculty of Medicine at Souss, and we arrived at the following interpretation.

Firstly, let us ask 'what is hysteria?'. P. Hardy defines it as:

a polysymptomatic infection affecting women (from 1 to 2% of women in France). It begins generally at about age 25, and is characterized by recurrent and lasting outbreaks, whose history is often confused. Accidents of conversion are only one element in a rich semiology which, against a background of anxiety and thymic lability, can also include spasms, tiredness, depression, pains, difficulties in digesting, menstrual and sexual problems. The duration of outbreaks can vary greatly, from a few days aphonia to fixed paralysis lasting for years.

The most important points are that the symptoms of hysteria mainly affect the interactive aspects of life (motility, sensitivity, speech, comprehension). They appear as neurological pathologies but do not conform to the laws of physiology and anatomy; instead they are in keeping with the idea the patient has of those laws.

Patients affect a remarkable lack of attention to the symptoms. They forget the loss of function they are suffering. This oversight is not a perceptive defect but a negation, which actually engenders the symptom. The patient forgets to see or to speak (Charcot). It is not the imitation of an illness but the expression of a specific conflict with the social environment. It is a psychic illness, using the imagination but by no means imaginary.

Most authors agree that hysteria is not a neurological disorder and is more akin to hypnotic suggestion. Charcot showed, over a century ago, that one can reproduce the symptoms of hysteria through hypnosis.

In current practice, two closely linked but distinct features of hysteria are usually differentiated, namely: physical expression (conversion proper) and disassociative reaction, which is not to be confused with the changes in personality observed in cases of schizophrenia. There is no fracture of the personality, but a split between the intact personality as a whole and a special state of consciousness (a specific mental state, as in hypnosis).

Other important points include: 1) the hysterical personality: which is characterized by a tendency to lie and to confabulate; 2) psychoplasticity; thanks to which morbid states are maintained and developed through auto- and hetero-suggestion; 3) a great dependence *vis à vis* the environment, the patient living only thanks to the efforts of others; passivity and infantilism; 4) the histrionic personality, which adjusts according to its audience, like an actor who assesses the mood of his public; 5) manipulative behaviour; 6) characteristic ways of thinking, notably seeking refuge in fantasy, rejecting reality, refusing to face facts, easily distracted.

The study covered all hysterical patients treated at the Monastir hospital over a two year period. It consists of 50 dossiers, which covered: weight, age, place of origin, profession, medical history, number of siblings, rank in sibling group, level of education, marital status, date at which the symptom first appeared, what triggered it off, nature of the symptom, its meaning and the secondary benefits sought.

The results were as follows: 90.5% of hysterics were women, of which 74% were under 25 years of age and 54% were between 16 and 25; the average age was 25 years. Average family size was 5.4 children. Rank in the sibling group: average 4.42. Profession: 38% had none; 19% were workers; 19% indeterminate (domestic servants?). Education: 28.6% had none; 28.6% primary only; 19% secondary; with 23.8% indeterminate. Marital status: 57% unmarried; 26% married; 16.67% indeterminate. Place of origin: 40.4% from an urban background; 45.2% semi-urban; 14.3% rural. Leisure activities: embroidery and sewing 4.76%; trips out of the home 2.4%; indeterminate 92.8%. Medical history: psychiatric 17%; surgical and medical 21% and 24% respectively; indeterminate 48%. Triggering events: interpersonal conflict 62% (family, husband, etc.); medical or surgical intervention 12%; death of parent 14%.

The profile of the hysteric that emerges is that of a young woman, about 21, unmarried, illiterate or poorly educated, from a semi-urban background, without any profession or with a poorly paid low-status job, the fourth child of a family of six children, without any previous psychiatric history. In most cases the triggering event would be an interpersonal conflict. We will see how this profile differs in almost every respect from that of the woman suffering from depression.

Depression

The study of depression presented was carried out at the Razi psychiatric hospital in Tunis by a group of psychiatrists attached to the hospital. Their data will be used but our own interpretation differs from theirs. The study covered 250 patients, all of whom had been incapacitated for a prolonged period by a chronic depressive state. But before considering the results of the study it is necessary to consider what comprises depression.

There are no clinical criteria for diagnosing depression; diagnosis is a question of clinical experience.

The illness presents as permanent sadness. The person feels devalued, guilty, hopeless, incapable of coping. She has no interest in her work (feels weak) or in her pastimes (no pleasure), or even in her family. Depression is characterized by lassitude, low blood pressure, slow psychomotor responses, and sometimes by anxiety, loss of appetite or morbid hunger. On the semiological level there is a somatic element and a subjective element.

The psychological mechanism

Studies of bereavement give some idea of the object relations of the depressed person. In bereavement (death of a loved one) two phases can be distinguished: 1) an immediate reaction; crying, wailing, etc; 2) a more or less extended period of depression referred to as the 'working out of bereavement' during which an affective disinvestment in the lost object can take place. During this period, the person turns away from reality, maintaining interior links with the lost loved one and thereby trying to keep him or her alive for a time. This period corresponds to the action of a mechanism of identification with the lost one, indicating a temporary regression to a narcissistic infantile stage. At the end of the period, the subject can detach him/herself from the lost object and become free again.

Depression also corresponds to an experience of loss of an object, sometimes real, more often subconscious. The lost subconscious object refers back to an internal object, the 'lost object' of the earliest object relations, which the child has to give up in the course of its development.

The loss of self-esteem can be explained by a very narrow regressive and narcissistic identification of the subject with this lost object, producing a feeling of emptiness. It is worth noting that if the subject had ambiguous feelings about the lost object (because of frustration at early stages in development or early disappointment of infantile narcissism) love for the object which cannot be given up seeks refuge in narcissistic identification, while hatred seeks refuge in a substitute object, in this case the self, by dragging it down, making it suffer, and taking sadistic satisfaction in this suffering.

In depression, we are thus talking about masochistic enjoyment, the sadistic impulse and destructive hatred originally aimed at the object is turned back upon the self. The notion of loss implies an imaginary destruction of the object, hence the feelings of guilt stemming from the super ego and the desire for self-destruction and death.

As noted above, the study covered 250 women, all of whom had been incapacitated for more than three months by a chronic depression. Of these women 64% were between 30 and 40-years-old; 16% were between 40 and 50;

90% were married. More than two thirds had two or three children; 87% came from poor backgrounds, work undeniably represented a form of social advancement for them; 78% came from the interior of the country, even though they worked in the capital. Nearly all had received a strictly traditional education, in conservative families in which the mother had never worked. 35.6% had received no, or only primary, education; 50.4% had some secondary education; 14% had received higher education. On average, the women had worked at their job for 14.5 years, and had started at 20. Only 55% had any professional qualifications: 25% were health auxiliaries; 21% were secretaries, and 9% were teachers. Most were state employees. Only 3% had any traceable psychiatric history (although this may be an underestimate); 37% had a history of gynaecological problems; 5% had undergone some surgical intervention; 18.5% had required medical intervention. Psychotic or neurotic personalities were very rare amongst the group; most of them seemed to be emotive, sensitive, rather introverted. The triggering factors described by the patients can be broken down as follows: domestic quarrel 57%, professional problems 5%, loss or illness of a loved one 20.3%; physical trauma 18.5%.

The typical profile that emerges is of a woman of 35, who has worked for over 15 years, from a poor and culturally traditional background, with some secondary education but no professional qualifications, a wife and the mother of two children.

Comments of psychiatrists who carried out the study

Patients regularly complained of a set of three symptoms, forming a syndrome: headaches, insomnia and changes in personality. It was the third of these – the change in personality – that most concerned both the patients and their family. The patient complains that she has become intensely irritable and quick tempered, reacting violently to any stimulus, whether physical or psychological (emotions, efforts, and so on) with the result that she gradually reduces the range of her activities and of her relationships, finding peace only by shutting herself in a darkened room.

This set of problems grows more serious over the years and is made worse by feelings of inadequacy and incompetence, and by constant self-depreciation. As her state of health and her relationships deteriorate, depression proper sets in. It is at this stage that, as a last resort, the first psychiatric consultation is sought, when the patience and capabilities of many general practitioners and other specialists have been worn out over months or even years. Psychiatric treatment, prescribing anti-depressive drugs and a long period of rest, has little effect either. The picture will remain unchanged for years. The inevitability of a return to work, after a two or three year period of extended leave, then raises the problem of an early retirement or some form of certification as an invalid.

Before commenting on these two studies, I would like to pose a general question. Do the mentally ill have a psychological make-up that is unbalanced independently of their social environment, or only in terms of the culture in which they live? My own opinion is, as the WHO has long suggested, that health is the outcome of successful adaptation. It is then necessary to recognize that an individual – in perhaps every case – is sick only in terms of a given culture, when the way they function clashes with the rules of that culture.

Our own hypothesis is that hysteria and depression are two characteristic strategies adopted by Tunisian women to manifest their lack of adaptation to a society whose official, social practice is modern and egalitarian, but whose interpersonal life is traditional and authoritarian.

What is a healthy (well adapted) individual in a modern industrial or post-industrial society? Janet Seely, in her excellent work, says that the healthy individual is the differentiated person, which she defines as:

> A well defined person in her own terms. She has the ability to separate intellectual and emotional function. She is rational and objective in taking decisions, and freely emotional when emotion is appropriate. She maintains a balance between the desire to be with others and the desire for individuality. Looking after her own interests does not mean she is selfish, and does not bring her into conflict with the interests of the group, but on the contrary is complementary to those interests. She can resist the group if it puts pressure on her to change but is tolerant of others' opinions when they differ from hers.

A glance at these points is sufficient to enable us to see that they in no way describe a person well adapted to the traditional culture of Tunisia. In this context, a well adapted person is what J. Seely calls 'undifferentiated', that is a person who bases her own opinions on those of the group, who takes her decisions according to pre-established norms rather than by making objective and rational choices, who melts into the group with no problems and without feeling any need to stand apart in order to know the boundaries of her own self. She will always defend the interests of her own group (tribe, clan, family or country) without trying to assess objectively the rights and wrongs of the situation. Her opinions change with that of the group and she does not tolerate differing opinions. Indeed, it would hardly be a caricature to say that there are no opinions to be held in such a situation, only norms, pre-established ways of saying what is right and wrong.

Our hypothesis is that this traditional ideology, which posits the primacy of the group over the individual, is the very essence of patriarchy. *Vis à vis* the father, who must retain all power for himself alone, all other individuals must be equal and similar, and must have no way of gaining any advantage over others through their own efforts, for that would threaten the system as a whole. As we know, social positions (amongst others those at work) are distributed on the basis of ascription rather than of achievement. Similarly, all power, including that of the father, is authority, that is to say, power exercised according to norms recognized by the social consensus. Authority differs from modern power (bargaining power) which can be defined as the individual capacity to achieve aimed-for results. While the basis of authority is social consensus, the basis of modern power, in its most finished form, is competence. In traditional society, only sex and age give access to authority; in modern society, competent young people and women can achieve power, that is to say the capacity to act upon others to achieve their own ends.

What, then, is the current situation in our Arab, and more specifically, Tunisian society? As we see it, the two rules (which in practice are contradictory) are in force simultaneously, and it is in the urban world that the contradiction is the most striking.

We believe that it is women – the greatest losers in traditional society – who wholeheartedly support the modern ideology, once they have truly discovered it, because it allows them to fight for their own desires, desires which the new norms have put on an equal footing with those of men. But it is women who also most threaten the authority of the father as we have defined it above. As women pose the greatest threat to the (patriarchal) system, the greatest pressure is brought to bear upon them, to prevent them from acceding to that power of achieving their own ends.

Our hypothesis is that the greatest stress to which Tunisian women are currently subjected stems from their exposure to two contradictory ideologies. One modern, insists that officially and legally they are the equals of men and can employ their abilities to gain access to power; the other, traditional and generally unspoken, but still dominating all interpersonal relations, continues to tell them, as it has done for centuries, that only age and membership of the male sex give access to authority, and what is worse, that it is an individual's sex, even more than their age, that now permits or forbids this access – which may even be a retrograde step compared to previous centuries.

Our hypothesis is that hysteria and depression are two ways available to women to express their rejection of the trap into which they have been forced.

The hysteric is a 'poorly differentiated' woman who plays the masculine game by denying (forgetting) her own desires which are repressed and reappear in the form of symptoms) and who seeks to act on her environment by manipulation and 'play-acting', in other words by a power over individuals which imitates masculine power. It is worth stressing the importance of 'giving the impression' in this context.

The depressed woman on the other hand is a well differentiated woman, but who has moved forward too fast in a traditional environment and hence finds that she is rejected and blocked by her milieu, and that her sense of self-esteem (her differentiation) is denied. She has no refuge other than depression. Our hypothesis is that the 'lost object' in this case is none other than the father, representative of the modern law who has not done justice by her. The fact that depression becomes untreatable indicates the hardening of the respective stances of the woman and her environment.

11. Yemenite Women: Employment and Future Challenges

Thaira A. Shaalan

Introduction

Women play a major role in building, maintaining and perpetuating society. Society, represented by the state, should, therefore, show due concern for women. In the Arab Republic of Yemen (North Yemen), laws have been promulgated to ensure women's participation in various fields of activity. In labour legislation and voting rights women are guaranteed equal status with men, as enshrined in the National Charter and Constitution.

Yemen existed in total isolation from the rest of the world under the rule of the Hamid El Din dynasty. With the Revolution of 26 September 1963, Yemen took the first steps on its long path of struggle.

This chapter discusses the issue of women and employment and the developments that took place in women's participation both in the civil service and in agriculture and the challenges still to be confronted until the year 2000. To trace the changing role of women since 1962, two areas were selected: 1) the modern state sector; and 2) the old system of agriculture to which the Yemenite population has, as a whole, been linked since time immemorial. I propose to focus on: 1) the social and economic background for women's work in Yemen; 2) fields of activity and labour laws; and 3) challenges confronting women in Yemen.

Women's work in Yemen: social and economic background

In order to gain an insight into the state of women today, it is necessary to review the changes which took place in Yemen from 1962.

Women in the urban areas of Yemen previously did not participate in any field of activity; they were deprived of any education. Before the Revolution, primary education was accessible only to boys.[1] In rural areas women constituted and still constitute an important force: they rear animals, carry water, collect fuel as well as participate in certain household industries.

Despite certain differences, life for women in Yemen had much in common with the conditions of life for other Arab women. Some researchers contend that by examining the actual reality of Arab women and their role in fostering the economic development of their societies, other factors pertaining to the emancipation of women at the present stage will be brought to light.[2] A factual description of women in Yemen, therefore, must necessarily be considered in the context of the far-reaching economic changes taking place in the society. Such changes have not occurred without a high price paid by the people of Yemen who struggled to put an end to decades of subjugation and darkness. Indeed, the mere acquisition of women's right to education was an accomplishment not to be undermined.

The Revolution helped close the gap between classes, and to provide the opportunity for a greater degree of social mobility. Yemen witnessed the emergence of new administrative structures. A modest network of services was first established. Another new development was a migratory movement out of Yemen. Emigration in search of work opportunities in other countries drained off a high percentage of the male labour force. Women remained in Yemen and still constitute the backbone of the productive force, mainly in the field of agriculture.

According to the 1986 census, there were 1,168,199 migrants from Yemen as against 1,234,000 in 1975. In 1982, the total number of emigrants exceeded the total labour force inside Yemen. According to the 1981 population census short and long term migrants totalled 1,396,123 and the domestic labour force 1,201,600. As most emigrants were from the rural area, the impact of a reduced labour force was largely felt in agriculture.[3] History will record that Yemenite women have borne the responsibility for production particularly in the agricultural sector where women have even tilled the soil.

Fields of activity and labour laws

Percentages cited in table 11.1 should be treated with caution and related to the size of the population and labour force. Preliminary results of the survey of houses and inhabitants undertaken in February 1986 showed that the sex ratio (male:female) of the population in Yemen was 97:100 as against 91:100 in the 1975 census.[4] The difference is attributed to large numbers of emigrants returning to Yemen.

Table 11.1
Number of females to males: 1986 Census

Description	Sex Distribution		
	Males	*Females*	*Total*
Population in Yemen	3,800,791	3,928,440	7,729,231
Migrants	804,007	364,192	1,168,199
Numbers added for technical & social considerations	42,512	334,234	376,734
Total population	*4,647,310*	*24,626,863*	*9,274,173*

In 1975, the results of the survey of houses and inhabitants revealed that the productive force in Yemen (total population above the age of ten less incapacitated persons) was estimated at 2,816,000 individuals or approximately 63% of the total population. Females in the labour force were estimated at approximately 1,502,000, or 53% of the force, as against 47% males. The labour force may in turn be divided into those who are not employed and refuse to work and those who are productive whether they are working or seeking work. Yemen's labour force is estimated at 1,127,600 or 39% of the total population over the age of ten.

According to the 1975 census, men in the labour force were estimated at 994,000 or 88.2% of the total as against 113,000 women or 11.2%.[5] The low percentage of female participation in the labour force indicated by the figures is because female labour in agriculture is unwaged and, therefore, despite its major economic significance, was not taken into account.

The high level of illiteracy among women, estimated at 97.2% in the 1975 census, is one cause of their low participation in activities of modern life. Table 11.2 shows the distribution of education levels among women.

Table 11.2
Education levels of Yemeni women

Level of Education	Percentage
Illiterate	97.20%
Read only	.70%
Read and write	1.40%
Primary	.20%
Preparatory	.05%
Secondary	.03%
University	.02%
Unspecified	.40%

Fields of activity involving women

The Civil Service

Before the 1962 Revolution women participated only in agricultural work but, as table 11.3 indicates, their participation in the civil service gradually increased in the post-1962 years, and between 1975 and 1983 their numbers more than doubled.

Table 11.3
Women in the Civil Service

Year	Total number of employees	Number of women	Percentage
1975	17,491	1,077	6.16%
1983	25,622	2,845	11.10%

Source: Ministry of Civil Service: A Statistical Study on Working Yemenite Women During the Period 1975–1983, p. 40.

During the years 1975–82, an average of 221 women joined the labour force each year. This is, however, only a small number despite the fact that labour laws provide for men and women to be employed in the same kind of job on equal terms.[6] The reason for this is that many women hold staunchly to old styles of living. The increased employment of women was concentrated in the Ministry of Education: a 45% increase; and the Ministry of Health: 13.5% increase. These two ministries seem to be especially attractive to women as they are seen to be more relevant to their social conditions. Furthermore both these ministries have played a leading role in the transitory period in which Yemen is living. Out of the total number of qualified women employed in the government sector in 1982, the percentage for the Ministry of Education was 48%; and 24% for the Ministry of Health; in 1983 it was 57.8% and 15.6% respectively.

On the other hand, women are totally absent from such fields as: physical education and veterinary medicine; also from the judiciary and law because they are legally prohibited from any profession related to either. Women are also banned from employment in the following areas: the President's secretariat general; office of prime minister; Bureau of Information and Guidance; corrective courts;[7] supreme court; Higher Judiciary Institute; police and related activities. Women are employed as cleaners and typists in various ministries of government bodies.

The agricultural sector

Agriculture is the main field for women's labour as well as for labour in general as it involves three quarters of the total labour force in Yemen; the remaining quarter is distributed between all other fields of activity.[8]

A 1983 study on Women's Participation in Economic Activities conducted by the Central Authority for Planning in the four governorates of Sanaa Taa'iz, Al Hudaida and Aab revealed that the percentage of women's participation in economic activities is higher than that for men. This is due to the high percentage of male labour emigration from the four governorates which accommodate the majority of the population of Yemen.

Male to female labour distribution in the rural areas of the same governorates was found to be 70% females and 30% males over the age of ten. Their distribution among the different employment categories was as follows: women employees over the age of ten, 62.86%; waged women, 10.61%; unwaged women, 86.34%; self-employed women 2.65%. Statistics revealed that 92% of women are working, as against 8% unemployed (job seekers, and those who do not wish to work). Of the total female labour force, 98.5% engage in agricultural activities.[9]

In rural areas, all household members participate in agricultural work, but younger women bear the brunt of it. The percentage of women engaged in agricultural activities is intensive in the lower age groups, falling somewhat in the 20–34 age group, then increasing again to reach its peak in the 40–44 age group after which there is a constant decline throughout the older age groups. The decline in participation of the 20–34 age groups is evidently due to fertility factors.[10]

Unlike in the case of men, women's participation in agriculture increases among the married. This is because a woman must work for her in-laws, and one of the positive attributes of a wife is a strong constitution. Payment of dowry to the bride's family is one of the conditions of marriage in rural Yemen; in return, the husband benefits from her labour on his land.[11] Despite the establishment of numerous modern projects in the rural areas for increasing agricultural production, however, no roles have been allocated to women. Similarly no campaigns have been launched to alert women as to the changes that could be induced as a result of their participation in economic activity, or the potential benefits to be reaped from the employment of women. No modern machinery was introduced to help women in their agricultural labour, and the domain of women's work remains untouched by any attempts to develop or modernize it.

In this respect, the case of Yemenite women is similar to that of women in other Arab countries. A study on the Sudan and Jordan, conducted by Mohamed Awad, revealed that although women constitute the greater part of the labour force, they have no part in decision making. Consequently, when technology was introduced to agriculture, it was geared to men's activities, and men alone were trained in the use of new technology; a fact that helped enhance the male role.[12]

Challenges facing Yemenite women

Women in Yemen have a peculiar status. They are responsible for agricultural production as well as for the life of the community in many villages. Advocates of backwardness are, however, championing campaigns in the cities to deprive women of education and work, and to impose the veil. But rural areas are not a fertile soil for such ideas as rural women are mostly unveiled and are the main force in agricultural production. These reactionary trends in Yemen will, therefore, remain of limited scope confined within the boundaries of the major cities. But women are responsible for responding to such campaigns and the choice to wear the veil is their own.

Despite the few rights, including education and work opportunities in certain modern sectors, women have obtained, we still see the majority of women employees in the public sector as well as in the modern sectors veiled. The challenges facing women in Yemen threaten to strip them of the few rights they enjoy, including representation and voting rights for the Peoples' Assembly and local councils, as well as the right to education. One of these challenges is the demand for the cancellation of co-education in primary schools. A positive response to this demand could have grave consequences for female education due to the scarcity of schools in general, and the lack of resources to build schools for girls in villages. As a result, the little education made available to girls will be once again eliminated. The demand to deny education to women is growing and echoed by the demand to bar women from university education, for sex segregation of university students and for imposing the veil on women students.

The main challenges that Yemenite women will face in the various fields of activities during the coming period may be summarized as follows:

1. The need for women's participation in all fields of activity.

2. The establishment of women's associations and unions in the different governorates rather than limit women's collective action to the family planning society located in Sanaa' Taa'iz and Al Hudaida.

3. To establish branches of the University of Sanaa' in the principal governorates, so that women students need not be deprived of pursuing their education because of their social circumstances. For example, when the Faculty of Education, Sanaa' University opened a branch in the city of Taa'iz, many students enrolled.

4. To adopt the principle of compulsory primary education for boys and girls.

5. To establish the principle of equality of opportunity in order to overcome: a) shortage of schools for girls; b) absence of vocational and technical schools for girls, which is one factor that limits women's work opportunities and confines them to the home and to the influences of tradition. Such a state is incompatible with the provisions of Article 4 of the Arab Convention No. 5 of 1976 on the employment of women which states that: 'Every effort should be made to provide equal opportunities to women . . . women should have equal access to education in all its stages, to guidance and vocational training before and after employment'.

Notes

1. Osman, Abdn. 'On Education and Social Change', *Al Ghad Magazine*, No. 2, 3rd year June 1977, p. 10.

2. Shaidolina, Louisa, 'Arab Women and Age', translated by Shawkat Youssif, Dar al-Jeel printing press, not dated, p. 48.

3. Al-Gaseer, Ahmed. 'The Effects of Emigration on the Social Structure in the Arab Republic of Yemen', *Al-Mustaqbil al-Arabi* magazine, No. 70, Dec. 1984, p. 119.

4. Central Authority for Planning, *Survey of Houses and Inhabitants*, Feb. 1986, Preliminary Results p. 3.

5. Ibid.

6. Al-Haj, Mohammed al-Godir, *Description of the Yemeni Labour Laws*, al-Katib al-Arabi Press, Damascus, undated, p. 81.

7. Ministry of Civil Service, 'A statistical study on working Yemeni women during the years 1975–83', p. 12.

8. Ibid.

9. Central Authority for Planning, 'A Study on Women's Participation in Economic Activities', p. 19.

10. Analysis of the 1975 survey for the distribution of the population by economic activity, p. 12.

11. Advisory group of the Central Authority for Planning, 'Women and Development in the Arab Republic of Yemen, 1983', p. 24.

12. Jalal al-Din, Mohamed al-Awad, 'Gender discrimination and its reflection on women's role in society: Jordan and Sudan', *Social Sciences*, Vol. 12, No. 3, Autumn 1984, p. 34.

12. Lebanese Women and Capitalist Cataclysm

Rima Sabban

The United Nations statistics and resolutions published before and after the Nairobi Conference[1] showed that women constitute the majority of the world's poor, unemployed and economically and socially disadvantaged. They provide two-thirds of the world's work force, receive only 5% of the world's income, and own less than 1% of the world's assets.[2] The growth indices of the male and female labour force, between 1970 and 1980, showed larger worker participation in the developing countries (120) than in the developed countries (113).[3] Most workers in developing countries live in critical situations. 'Today, 570 million women are living in conditions of grinding poverty, malnutrition, disease and with no protected water supplies'.[4]

Women have been historically impoverished and continuously exploited. A study published by DAWN (Development Alternatives with Women in a New Era) – a group of women scholars, mostly from the Third World – spells out the exploitation and impoverishment of Third World women. It states that these countries, despite their differences in culture, history and political institutions, all share problems of backwardness and impoverishment, partly because of the colonial system that not only drained their resources and wealth, but also 'created export enclaves in agriculture, mining and other sectors, suppressed the manufacturing potential of the colonies, destroyed traditional crafts through imports of manufactured goods and transferred formerly self-supporting communities through forced commercialization and the introduction of private property in land.' In addition women's impoverishment,

> has been documented: their loss of traditional land-use rights with the introduction of private property in land; their displacement from employment and loss of income as traditional manufactures decayed; and the heavy burden they had to assume with meagre resources to feed and care for children, the aged and infirm as men migrated or were conscripted into forced labour. The colonial era thus not only laid the basis for the particular position of Third World countries in the world economy but added further layers to women's social, economic and political subordination.[5]

DAWN and most Third World women representing non-governmental organizations at the Nairobi Conference projected this image of women's exploitation and related it to the world economic system; this system was then heavily criticized and some called for a new economic order. Andriamanjato of Madagascar and Krishnan of India submitted a paper entitled 'Women and NIEO' (New International Economic Order) and insisted that 'colonialism and neo-colonialism are at the heart of Third World women's exploitation. Colonialism did not bring civilization; on the contrary, it forced degradation'. If the Third World asked the former colonizer to pay 'an interest on the capital that they utilized, it is they who would be bankrupt and not us, the developing countries.'[6]

The subject of this chapter arises from this feeling expressed by Third World women at the largest women's world conference ever held. I have chosen Lebanon as the area for illustration, both historically and currently excluding the period of the war (1975–83). The impact that the integration of Lebanon in the world economic system had on Lebanese women is considered, using the dependency approach as a theoretical framework, and arguing that this integration distorted the whole economy of Lebanon, marginalized women's role in production and mystified their role in reproduction. This chapter also asserts that this integration has deformed the development of social strata and classes; inhibited the growth of a national industrial bourgeoisie, and aided the growth of a comprador bourgeoisie, a class whose women perform an important role in perpetuating the system. Finally, it looks at the impact that the substructure, created by this integration, has had on the superstructure, in such contexts as family, education, culture, and so on.

Theoretical setting

To discuss the impact of the integration of Lebanon into the WCS (World Capitalist System as most dependency literature calls it) it is necessary to provide a definition of that system and the assumptions behind it, identifying its relationship to women's exploitation, and finally laying down the framework that relates all these theoretical abstractions to the concrete case of Lebanese women.

Dependency, according to Dos Santos, means 'a situation in which the economy of certain countries is conditioned by the development and expansion of another economy to which the former is subjected.'[7] Thus a fundamental assumption of dependency theory is that the continued development of the industrialized capitalist countries is possible only at the expense of continued impoverishment in the economically underdeveloped countries of the periphery. André Gunder Frank, the most widely quoted dependency theorist, states this most succinctly.

> Economic development and underdevelopment are the opposite faces of the same coin. Both are the necessary result and contemporary manifestation of internal contradictions in the world capitalistic system . . . One and the same historical process of the expansion and development of capitalism throughout the world has simultaneously generated and continues to generate both economic development and structural underdevelopment.[8]

The dependency approach deals with development and underdevelopment by assuming that there is one unified world system – the international capitalist system. This system is structurally divided into two types of countries: the centre and the periphery. The former is composed of the now advanced capitalist countries, the latter of various less-developed and economically backward countries. Each of these countries fulfills a role in the international division of labour. Countries in the periphery were previously colonies and are now primary raw material producers. Thus the historical legacy is the present structural dependency.

In its socio-political form, dependency also means the existence of certain domestic social classes (for example, the comprador bourgeoisie) integrally linked to the mechanism of the international capitalist system. They are willing, but not necessarily subordinate, partners in what Samir Amin called 'the international class alliances'.[9] This is the social class which, because of its dominant position in the economic and political system, facilitates foreign capital domination and consolidates the country's integration into the world capitalist system.

In essence, dependency analysis focuses on the internal economic and socio-political expressions of the world capitalist system. That is to say, dependency is not a mere deterministic influence on the external forces, rather, in a situation of dependency, the external is politically, socially and culturally internalized. Thus, an understanding of the internal structure of dependency is one of the most challenging aspects of dependency analysis. Susanne Boderheimer writes that, 'dependency doesn't mean simply external domination, unilaterally superimposed from abroad'.[10] It remains to be pointed out, however, that Third World societies have been incorporated into the expanding capitalist world economic system. This has not only produced external reliance but has also had profound internal effects which, in turn, independently reproduced dependency.

Dependency structures, therefore, affected Third World women and deformed their indigenous development as it did to all other social strata. This deformation is twofold; the first is on the level of capitalism as a holistic system, based on the exploitation of women, marginalization of female labour and its relation to the means of production, and the mystification[11] of their role in reproduction. The second deformation is on the level of the periphery that embodies a 'cataclysmic' capitalism, that is, an underdeveloped capitalism, unable to industrialize, modernize or integrate its society independently. This capitalism enforces the old traditional values in a mystified way, that usually exploits the basis of sex and race, family ties and kinship, as is the case in Lebanon. Peripheral capitalism is also in a continuous state of chaos and disintegration where women, especially those not integrated in the WCS, have to carry heavier economic, political, social, and cultural burdens. They are economically marginalized, politically dismissed, socially exploited and culturally subdued.

Capitalism in its very historical mode of development embodies the seeds of women's exploitation. In the words of Saffiotti, a Brazilian woman who studied the impact of capitalism on women:

> The circumstances surrounding the birth of capitalism were extremely inauspicious for women. The process of individualization that commenced with the capitalist mode of production put women at a twofold disadvantage socially. The superstructure traditionally underrated women's capacities, and created myths of male supremacy to justify itself and the existing social order. Secondly, at a more basic level, as the productive forces developed, women became progressively more peripheral to the system of production.[12]

This process of marginalization of women's labour is based on their use as reserve labour. In the introduction to *Women in Class Society*, Leacock summed it up nicely: 'it can be used or cast aside in accordance with economic exigencies.'[13]

On the level of the Third World's underdeveloped capitalism, the same process has happened to women, but in a more crucial way. In as much as the underdeveloped countries are continuously deprived, their surplus capital is flying outside, their labour is exploited cheaply and the capitalist cycle is never completed, they will continuously regenerate the subsistent economy. Women in these situations are pushed to work, albeit in a marginalized context, and under traditional subjective and objective conditions that are continuously enforced by the underdeveloped capitalism. In addition, they earn less and do the peripheral work. At the same time, the dependency structure widens the socio-economic gap among the integrated and non-integrated social classes and strata. Rich women are used to add to the mystification of women's exploitation and to cast out and alienate the massive number of women, who are deprived of basic needs (food, education), from an indigenous revolutionary feminist movement. Also, the dominant social values and culture are those of the dominant classes that are traditional (feudal and sectarian in the case of Lebanon). On the other hand, they allow modern behaviour to exist as a bridge with the centre countries, or a home for the flow of capital and the multinational corporations. In this situation women are torn between modern and traditional values, and many pay the price of this cataclysm with their lives.[14]

Lebanon is a dependent country that has twice been integrated into the international division of labour. First, as a result of its initial encounter with Western colonialist power in the mid-1800's, as a producer of raw materials. Second, after World War II, when the Lebanese economy carried out a wider regional role as a service economy. This historically enforced integration, forcefully perpetuated through a dependent internal structure, had its effect on Lebanese women and distorted their natural development in most aspects of life.

Historical framework

The initial economic integration meant that on the one hand, Lebanon became increasingly a crossroads country facilitating European trade with the Arab East, and a market for commodities manufactured in the industrialized countries. On the other hand, and perhaps more important, was its transformation into a single commodity, producing and cultivating economic 'monoculture'. It specialized in raw silk, exclusively exported to Europe and particularly France. Indeed the silk plantations, heavily financed by French capital, experienced a phenomenal growth between 1880 and 1919. Lebanon's virtually exclusive dependency on the production of raw silk was such that by 1910, 180,000 Lebanese, representing 60% of the whole population, engaged in this trade.[15] Export figures also highlight the trend: in 1835, Lebanon exported only 25% of its silk to the world market, by 1861, 66% was exported to France. By 1985, silk production constituted 45% of Lebanon's entire gross national product (GNP).[16]

Lebanese women, especially those who lived in the mountains, were deeply involved in silk production: they fed the silk worms, cared for the cocoons, and kept them warm. 'Lebanese women, especially the poor ones, used to put these cocoons in their pillows, and in tissue bags inside their bodice to keep them warm.'[17] Jacqueline Des Villettes, in her book, *La Vie des Femmes dans un Village Maronite Libanais*, describes how in Ain El Kharoube, silk production was a family enterprise; women were responsible for caring for the cocoons during the 35 days of their development. When the time came to collect the silk from the cocoon, groups of women would sit on the ground and work together. When the work was done, the hostess distributed sweets and preserves.[18] When silk production developed outside the homes some women went to earn their living in the factories. Most of the silk refining was supervised by women.[19]

At that time, out of a total of 20,000 industrial workers 4,200 were women and 2,400 were children. According to the League of Nations records a total of 79,000 peasants worked in the fields; of these 17,000 were women and 13,000 were children. Women workers constituted 22% out of the overall working force in Lebanon while women and children together constituted 35%.[20]

However much Lebanese women contributed to the internal mode of production and the external silk trade, their labour was marginalized and denied social value. They were hired only because of their low cost, and as economic dependants of the male labour power. Marx explains this process very clearly.

> In so far as machinery dispenses with muscular power, it becomes a means of employing labourers of slight muscular strength, and those whose bodily development is incomplete, but whose limbs are all the more supple. The labour of women and children was, therefore, the first thing sought for by capitalists who used machinery . . . The value of labour-power was determined, not only by the labour-time necessary to maintain the individual adult labourer, but also by that necessary to maintain his family. Machinery, by throwing every member of that family on the labour-market, spreads the value of the man's labour-power over his whole family. It thus depreciates his labour power. To purchase the labour-power of a family of four workers may, perhaps, cost more than it formerly did to purchase the

labour-power of the head of the family, but, in return, four days' labour takes the place of one, and their price falls in proportion to the excess of the surplus-labour of four over the surplus-labour of one . . . Previously, the workman sold his own labour-power, which he disposed of nominally as a free agent. Now he sells wife and child. He has become a slave dealer.[21]

In Lebanon, a couple of Lebanese families became the slave dealers, selling cheaply to all other Lebanese families in the French market. The price of one kilogram of silk cocoons in Lebanon was seven to nine French francs (FF), but in Paris it was 165 to 195 FF; French silk sold in Paris fetched only 41 to 43 FF.[22]

Women produced one-third of the Lebanese silk, were paid the lowest wages and were unable to improve their material position. They worked in order to maintain the family financial base; their work did not improve their status either in the family or in society. The introduction of Lebanon to the WCS fortified the traditional substructure and superstructure, giving it a broader horizon for exploitation, increasing alienation and fetishism and, at the same time, making conditions easier for international capital.

The old feudal lords became the new entrepreneurs; they emerged with their families economically, politically, socially and culturally stronger. This gave the patriarchal hierarchy more autonomy. Men were favoured in every facet of their lives, but this was not merely a reflection of male domination over female. It was a main feature of the backward Lebanese economic system that shifted from dependence on the Turks to dependence on the French, without the opportunity to become liberated from this dependency, or to liberate its indigenous productive forces, men and women, on either economic, political, cultural or social levels.[23] Not surprisingly, when world demand for silk declined, and when, after World War I, French capital and markets were no longer available, the Lebanese women were the first to suffer the consequences. Because of Lebanon's complete dependency on foreign markets and capital, it went into virtual financial bankruptcy and economic chaos that also produced massive migration. Between 1900 and 1914, the number of those emigrating reached 15,000 per year. As a result in the decline of the silk industry, one village alone, 'Beit Shebab', an exclusively silk-producing village, lost 3,000 inhabitants, and the number of workers in the city of Tripoli fell from 14,000 to 3,500.[24] Lebanese women not only had to suffer the poor state of the economy, being the first to be out of work, but also the socio-cultural consequences where any economic depression leads to more oppression of women in a male dominated society. So when men had to migrate looking for jobs, women became fully responsible for the house, children, land and animals.[25] This seemingly autonomous situation rarely gave them real autonomy, because they were tied up with the old social values, reinforced by the emerging capitalist structure. Again, Lebanese women, as the most deprived, had to face up to the most negative consequences. In education for example, in 1928, there were 6,263 male students compared to 1,002 female students. This number decreased after the depression to 710 female students, compared to 5,410 males,[26] a decrease of 20% of male, and 70% of female students.

The integration of Lebanon into the WCS, therefore, created a new class of comprador bourgeoisie while eliminating the few emerging industrial bourgeoisie who were attempting to set up an indigenous textile industry. The number of commercial and financial families increased rapidly from 34 in 1910 to over 200 in 1927.[27] Most of these were commercial agents and middlemen engaged in financial activities intrinsically linked to the mechanism of the international division of labour.

Women, as a sex, are exploited by the very structure of the capitalist system; and, whereas in some dependency theory literature they are treated as non-integrated into the world system, women are, in fact, integrated as a class. Women of the emerging comprador bourgeoisie played, and still play, a prominent role in perpetuating this system. Their role is manifest at the level of superstructure: culture, social values, behaviour, education, women's organizations and so on. These women serve as the propaganda agents for this system. Educated in foreign missionary schools they then started their own institutions on the very basic ideologies of this system, that is, Orientalism. Suad Joseph, a Lebanese social scientist addressed this issue:

> Orientalism, sexism, and certain feminist approaches confined their consideration of Middle Eastern women to a limited discussion of veils, honor and shame, kinship, cousin right, polygamy, and Islam.[28] No wonder that the major concern of the women's movement at that time was the veil more than anything else.[29]

In addition, all women's movements at that time emerged in the cities, among the most privileged women who looked on these organizations as representing a kind of social prestige, and a pastime.[30] These privileged women benefited from the system and saw no need to change it. To them, women's liberation was a fashion they imported, as they did their perfume, to be worn occasionally to show off.[31] These spoilt daughters of the world capitalist system were partly responsible for the problems with which the indigenous, poor Lebanese women had to struggle. They helped to increase the mystifications already implanted by the initial integration of Lebanon in WCS, and the distorted structure that it established. How did this distorted structure develop? What were its impacts on Lebanese women from its inception until the eve of the civil war?

Lebanese women at the apogee of capitalism: 1920s–1975

During the period 1920 to 1940, Lebanon's link to the world capitalist system was the weakest it had been since its initial integration in the middle of the 19th century. This 20-year period allowed a degree of autonomous economic development to occur. Following World War II, however, Lebanon was reintegrated into the new international division of labour on a new basis. This time it was no longer parochially confined to being a raw material-producing country, but gradually became an intermediary economy with a wider regional role. Abdallah Bouhabib, the current Lebanese Ambassador to the United States, described this period in the following terms:

> Before World War II, there were fewer than half a dozen American businessmen in Beirut, but after 1945, they began to arrive in waves. By 1960, a large number of American business firms, including Tapline and the Mediterranean Refining Co. (Medrico) had become established in Lebanon. In the mid-1960s, there were 355 American business offices in Beirut. There were also 60 social and educational institutions (schools, clubs, etc.).[32]

As a result, since 1950, Lebanon has experienced two types of interrelated dependency: 1) direct economic dependency; and 2) trade dependency. The service and the financial sectors in Lebanon are the most strategic arms of the national economy, and it is these sectors that are completely controlled by international monopoly capital. Similarly,

> The lopsided economic development of Lebanon is a consequence of its regional political–economic role. The country is a conduit not only of oil flowing from the east Arab hinterland, but also for the collection and export of Arab oil-based capital to the Euro-American money markets. Eighty-five per cent of all deposits in Lebanon banks are with foreign owned or foreign controlled banks operating in Lebanon. Four of the five largest banks in the country are branches of foreign metropolitan banks. These capital transfers have contributed importantly to Euro-dollar holdings in Europe.[33]

The financial sector contributed 62% of the GNP by 1962, and 70% by 1970. In 1975, there were 114 banks and financial affiliates.[34] Total bank deposits grew from LL2.15 million in 1950 to well over LL eight billion in 1974, an incredible 38-fold increase in 25 years. In 1950 total deposits constituted 20% of the total national income, whereas in 1970 it accounted for 105%.[35] According to Salim Nasr:

> The foreign dominated banking sector was taking away credits and resources that could have contributed to the growth of the national economy by investing 40 to 50 per cent of its resources outside Lebanon over the 1970–74 period. The foreign dominated banks have transferred to their central headquarters or to the international financial market more than half of the savings accumulated . . . , equivalent to between 50 and 60 per cent of the Lebanese gross domestic product.[36]

Along with such direct economic dependency, Lebanon experienced trade dependency. Foreign trade has consistently played a predominant role in the Lebanese economy which, alone, generated 31% of the entire GNP.[37] Indeed, imports increased from 34.8% of the GNP in 1967 to 53.6% in 1973. Lebanon's major trade partners were the United States, Britain, France, Italy, and Japan, accounting for nearly 75% of trade in 1975.[38]

In sum, Lebanon's economic integration into the world capitalist system had produced a number of internal structural distortions: 1) the hypertrophic growth of unproductive economic activities; 2) the extreme sectoral unevenness and maldistribution of income; 3) economic disarticulation; and

4) the blocking of growth and the inability to achieve autocentric development. These were the internal manifestations of Lebanon's dependency which created a weak and vulnerable economic structure unable to sustain itself once the dominant capitalist countries were no longer in need of its intermediary function.

The status of Lebanese women, who were by social definition feeble and dependent, was particularly denigrated at a time when the country was weak and vulnerable. What happened to them under these conditions of internal structural distortion and economic dependence? How were they affected?

The effects were manifold – economic, political, social, cultural – but here the argument largely focuses on those effects relating to the socio-economic substructure. Some of these impacts at the level of superstructure (education, culture, family) will be briefly addressed, assuming that the effects of capitalism on the two levels, and the dialectical relation between them, are equally important, especially when dealing with the exploitation of women. The aim of this chapter is not to emphasize the effects at the level of the superstructure as such. It is used only as an illustrative model to reflect the dynamic interaction between super- and substructure, on the one hand, and with external factors (the World Capitalist System) on the other.

First, the major impact of the distorted economic structure was projected on women's labour. According to the ILO, the level of Lebanese women's involvement in the labour force had decreased by 3.80% between the years 1950–70;[39] there had also been a dramatic decrease in their involvement in agriculture. In 1950, 76.2% of the female labour force was in agriculture, dropping to 23.6% in 1970.[40] This substantial decrease was due to the lopsided economy developed by the WCS, where more than two-thirds of the population involved in agriculture received less than one-third of the GNP, while the remaining one-third, who were involved in services, received two-thirds of the national wealth.[41] The only remarkable increase was in the service sector, where, in 1950, women's involvement was only 15.3%; by 1970 it was 56.4%.[42] A more detailed analysis, based on the type of work these women were doing, in relation to their age and family status will illustrate one of the highlighted assumptions of this paper, i.e. the effect of capitalism in marginalizing women's role in production.

Second, this lopsided economy and marginalization of women's role in production inhibits the growth and development of women's potential as a productive force, and is increasingly reproducing them as a peripheral social stratum, illiterate, unskilled, and impoverished.

Between 1950 and 1970 the Lebanese female labour force had more than doubled from 51,000 to 112,000.[43] Summing up the situation of Lebanese women in the work force in the early 1970s Irene Lorfing said:

Between 1972 and 1975, women in Lebanon represented 48.1% of the total population. The economically active women represented 17.5% of the female population, and 18.4% of the total labor force. The majority of the employed females were aged between 20 and 25 years. In 1972, 7% of the married women were employed. The largest groups of working women were: agricultural workers 22.6%, servant 22.5%, professionals (mostly teachers) 21.3%, industrial workers 19.6% and office employees 10.3%. Female occupations in Lebanon are traditional. Women work in jobs that are seen to benefit their sex. In 1972, 77% of the professional women were teachers; 61.6% of the women working in the commercial sector were secretaries and typists; 66.9% of those working in services were servants; and 69.5% of the women industrial workers were employed in the textile or tailoring industries. In the agricultural sector, women were classified as unskilled workers.[44]

The underlying causes of this peripheralization and marginalization of women's work and their relations of production[45] go back to the process of urbanization and development of Beirut as a centre or core for the flow of foreign capital, with the country as a whole a periphery.[46] Beirut and its suburbs constitute 75% of the population.[47] These people removed from the rural areas to the city, following the concentration of capital, lived in slums, and constituted the 'poverty belt', to which most comprehensive analyses of the Lebanese civil war give the primary emphasis. Women are among these peasants removed from their land and precapitalist mode of production to be dumped in the city. A study led by S. Nasr in 1974, found that the majority of unskilled and female labour in the industrial and service sectors were from this poverty belt.[48] While to quote Irene Lorfing again:

> One out of five industrial workers is a woman, usually young, single with minimal education and skills, and most often a recent migrant from the remote rural areas of south Lebanon or the Beqa'a Valley. These workers come from large families and are compelled to work in order to supplement familial income.[49]

The same facts were confirmed by M. Chamie, in 1980. She found that 83% of Lebanese female workers (10 to 50 years of age) were unmarried; 73% of these were below 25-years-old; 70% of them had worked before the age of 17; and of these 31% had started work before the age of 14.[50]

The work performed by these women comprises the primitive manufacturing jobs that Karl Marx referred to when addressing the issue of alienation of labour. Observation of women's tasks on the production line in some semi-mechanized industries, reveal that female workers' 'tasks' are situated at the beginning of the line for feeding the machine and at its end for checking the quality of the produce and ultimately packing. They are not allowed to touch the machine or fix it; this task is reserved for men. When employers were asked why they preferred women to men in these posts, the majority said that men are not to be trusted with surveillance, because they lack patience and dexterity. Employers also said that although mechanization may take over the place of many men and women workers, women will always be needed at the initial and final stage. Moreover, they insisted that they prefer young women, around age 18, because they are more trainable and patient.[51] When women at a clothes manufacturing plant were asked about their working conditions (in addition to noisy machines, bad ventilation and lighting and overcrowding) they voiced common complaints:

> In addition to family problems caused by their absence from home, are low pay, fatigue and inadequate transportation. This double burden imposed on working women is mentioned by most married workers (78%), who say that household chores consume most of their free time, a situation also found among 31% of the single. The majority of the workers indicate spending most of their free time in activities in and around the house.[52]

Third, the sectoral unevenness and maldistribution of income that benefited a tiny social class (4% of wealthy families receive 32% of the GNP),[53] integrated into the WCS on a feudal basis, affected Lebanese women by widening the social gap between the classes, especially between women. It also reinforced the traditional substructure and superstructure of women's exploitation (the family) preventing women from developing independently.

These three major distortions that affected Lebanese women on the level of substructure are characteristic of underdeveloped capitalist systems, although some can be found in most industrialized countries.

Reinforcement of the family structure on the levels of substructures and superstructures was well argued by K. and S. Farsoun. They first highlighted how the integration of Lebanon in the WCS enforced the traditional family structure (feudal) economically and politically, and identified the causes from their own empirical study. They concluded that:

> In Lebanon, it is the extended family which is structurally isolated, and in it are enmeshed and submerged nuclear units which interact intensively. The nuclear family system of the United States and other nations like it is adapted to a modern capitalist industrial economy needing mobile labor, and, until recently, expanding to allow for upward social mobility. In contrast, the extended family system of Lebanon is an adaptation to a neo-colonial economy which concentrates wealth, power and jobs in a single urban center and a tiny ruling class, in which a large segment is self employed in small enterprises (family firms), which hires on particularistic criteria (family and patronage) from among many able competitors, and which creates new jobs at a slow rate relative to population increase.[54]

This deformed and backward family structure has been emphasized by many socio-political writers who represent different approaches, among them functionalist and Marxist theorists. Suad Joseph provides a good overview of the literature on this matter.[55]

This family structure is reflected in the wide social gap that typifies Lebanese society – a gap that is almost impossible to diminish if Lebanon continues to follow the same underdeveloped capitalist trend.

In briefly describing this social gap I shall limit myself to a categorization of the integrated bourgeoisie.

A new, comprador bourgeoisie eventually emerged from the new economic activities. Unlike the traditional and agrarian bourgeoisie, these new classes had considerable links with the international sources of finance and technology, and were, therefore, more interested in preserving Lebanon's new peripheral function in the division of labour. The emergence of the new commercial and financial bourgeoisie, however, did not negate the political dominance of the traditional and agrarian capitalists; both the new and the old bourgeoisie have coexisted amicably and were also joined by the upper segments of the middle classes. Indeed, the new classifications of Lebanon's bourgeoisie become material in nature, such as commercial, industrial, and agricultural bourgeoisie. In addition, there are considerable diversities within each of these subclasses. For instance, the agricultural and real-estate bourgeoisie can be divided into four types: 1) the absentee agricultural bourgeoisie, who are also merchants living in the cities; 2) the service comprador bourgeoisie, who had made a considerable investment in the agricultural sector; 3) the remnant of the old feudal families who continued to constitute an important stratum of the dominant political élites in Lebanon; and 4) the integrated classes, classified here as the rich immigrant Lebanese, high ranking government officials, and professionals.

In the 1970s, these classes, which the Farsouns, adopting Gunder Frank's term, called the 'lumpen bourgeoisie' enjoyed an average per capita income of $3,680, while 50% of the Lebanese labour force earned only $166,[56] that is, a difference of $3,514. This means that the annual average income for each member of this lumpen bourgeoisie was 25 times that earned by a worker.

A more sophisticated categorization can be drawn for the Lebanese women integrated into the WCS. Despite the dearth of published studies on the subject, I found a book, *Women of Business and Society*, that helped trace some characteristics of these women. It provides a short summary of the life and career of the 100 most famous Lebanese women in the emerging business life of the country. A picture of each woman accompanies the summary, reflecting her successful and happy career. Although the book is concerned to sell these good business women and wives in the market, I found it useful in reflecting some features of these integrated women.

1. Most were from well-known Lebanese families integrated in the WCS. For example, five were Khourys, four were Boustanys. Many were from the remnants of such old feudal families as, for example; Jumblat, Eddé, Salha, al-Khalil, Sursok, Salaam.

2. Their material position, ownership and identification with the business world reflected their marginalization: 50% are shop owners, mostly of art, clothes, and furniture shops.

3. The type of prestige, in which they took pride and with which they identified, reflected their personal and psychological dependence on the patriarchal, male-dominated system characteristic of their social background: 30% were wives of famous businessmen; 30% came to business life as a result of their husband's death, or of a family inheritance.

4. Their religious and sectarian allegiances reflected their inheritance and the enforcement of the sectarian, corrupt Lebanese system: 65% were Christian, mostly Maronite; 25% Muslim Sunnite, and 10% Muslim Shiite.

In short, all these contending aspects of Lebanese society's substructure have affected its superstructure in different ways that enforced dependency, and the exploitation and marginalization of women. In education, this dependency created a dependent educational system, built on the legacy of the colonial system. The four biggest and most famous universities are foreign owned. One is a women's school that perpetuates the system in its very definition. An article on the establishment of Beirut College for Women states that:

> In 1866 Dr Henry Jessup was authorized to make an appeal to the Churches in America for funds to erect a suitable building and with the dedication of this building in 1866 another epoch in women's education began.[57]

From this College, the Institute for Women's Studies in the Arab World was established in the late 1970s. This Institute is very prolific in its writings and publications on Arab women, but financially it is dependent on the Ford Foundation, and the writings reflect Western ideology: modernization and political development. Irene Lorfing concluded among her suggested solutions to the problems of women's work, 'Business organizations and industries should be helped, materially and technically, to institute on-the-job training services for their female employees'.[58]

Another aspect of education is its bias towards the country's core centre. There are 1.6% illiterate women in Beirut, 54% in the suburbs, and 72.7% in the rural areas.[59] The figures are similar for other areas of the superstructure such as the media, women's organizations and so on.

Finally, it may be asked what can be done to abolish the injustices that Lebanese women, especially those not integrated into the WCS, are facing? Dependency literature provided some answers, such as socialism. Third World women at the Nairobi Conference also attempted to give some answers. It is, however, a complex matter because the struggle itself is still mystified and exacerbated by the many contradictions and complications of the capitalist system, internally as well as externally.

Notes

1. The Nairobi Conference ended the women's decade declared by the UN in 1975. Approximately 8,000 women attended.
2. A petition to the UN conference by the International Wages for Housework Campaign, entitled 'A Petition for all Women To All Governments, states: 'Whereas women do $\frac{2}{3}$ of the world's work, we receive only 5% assets. Whereas women are the poorer sex, and Black and Third World women are the poorest of all, the poorer we are the more work we are forced to do. Whereas women, with the help of children, grow at least $\frac{1}{2}$ of the world's food, yet we are denied the right to the technology of our choice. Whereas women do the work of caring for children, we are often threatened with the loss of child custody. Whereas because of women's pressure internationally, the United Nations has called all governments to count 'the contribution of the unpaid work that women do in the farms, at home and in other fields'. (UN Decade for Women Draft Programme of Action, 1980.) In *Connexions*, No. 17–18, Summer/Fall 1985, p. 28. See also *All Work and No Pay; Women, Housework and the Wages Due*, (ed.) Wendy Edmond and Suzie Flemming; *The Power of Women and the Subversion of*

the Community, Selma James and Mariarosa Dalla Costa. Both Falling Wall Press, Bristol, England.

3. *United Nations, World Survey On the Role of Women in Development*; Report of the Secretary General, Nairobi, 15–26 July 1985, Table 4, p. 79.

4. 'The One Trillion Dollar Question', *Connexions*, op. cit., p. 27.

5. Claire Slatter and Sally Murray, a summary of *Development, Crisis And Alternative Visions: Third World Women's Perspectives*; DAWN (Development Alternatives with Women in a New Era), Institute of Social Studies Trust (ISST), New Delhi, India.

6. *Connexions*, op. cit., p. 26.

7. Theodore Dos Santos, 'The Structure of Dependence', *American Economic Review*, Vol. 60, No. 2, 1970, p. 231.

8. André Gunder Frank, *Capitalism and Underdevelopment in Latin America*, p. 9.

9. Samir Amin, *Unequal Development*, p. 294.

10. S. Bodenheimer, 'The Ideology of Developmentalism', *BJS*, 15:1970, p. 127.

11. The term mystification of women's exploitation is used as in Marxist literature on women, and the structuralist school of dependency. It may seem that only men and women's close relatives exploit them; it is not only them, but the agents of the world capital, i.e. the world capitalist companies, enterprises and multinational corporations.

12. Heleieth I. B. Saffioti, *Women in Class Society*, p. 44.

13. Ibid.

14. Police records in Third World countries are an important reference for crimes, especially crimes of honour, where women have been chastized for social values that they were not responsible for.

15. 'The Financial Authoritarian Class', *Al-Tariq*, No. 4, 1979, p. 25. Also Claude Dubar and Salim Nasr, *Les Classes Sociales au Liban*, p. 52.

16. Ibid., pp. 52, 53.

17. Maurice Shehab, *Role of Lebanon in the History of Silk*, p. 38.

18. Jacqueline Des Villettes, *La Vie des Femmes dans un Village Maronite Libanais*, p. 103.

19. Massoud Daher, *Social History of Lebanon: 1914–1926*, p. 236.

20. Ibid., p. 236.

21. Karl Marx, *Capital*, Volume 1, pp. 394–6.

22. Massoud Daher, op. cit., p. 104.

23. Ibid., p. 239.

24. IRFED Commission, *Besoins et Possibilités de Développement du Liban*, and *Al-Tariq*, No. 4, 1979, p. 29.

25. An old Druze woman I knew in Beirut had to live in this situation. After her husband migrated to Brazil, she had to take care of three children, a small olive industry and olive trees. As a young attractive woman, living alone in a small village, she had to endure sexual harassment from the males of the community. She had to resist, not from choice, but also, because she was a mother who could have paid with her life as a punishment for adultery. Someone reported gossip to her husband, who divorced her from far away, without any inquiry. Poor Shahla found herself in the streets of Beirut, in the slums, with the eldest of her children only seven years-old.

26. Massoud Daher, op. cit., p. 239.

27. Dubar and Nasr, op. cit., pp. 57–8.

28. Suad Joseph, 'Working Class Women's Networks in a Sectarian State: A Political Paradox', *American Ethnological Society*, 1983, p. 3.

29. The first Lebanese women's organization was YWM (Young Muslim Women), established in 1880. Removing the veil was their major concern. They had a very active social life in the Turkish Palaces, and knew more Turkish than Arab history. The Christian aristocratic women did not play any important role politically or culturally. All their concern was focused on consumption. They appeared at cocktail parties wearing the latest fashions from Paris; made from pure silk that had been woven by poor women of the mountains and sold cheaply to the French manufacturers. Massoud Daher, op. cit., p. 240.

30. Some Lebanese women of the Sursok family maintained some cultural and social work interests; they were called 'Queens of Orient', where in their palaces 'kings, princes, and

princesses of the world were welcomed for life and joy'. Iskander Riyashi, *al-Ayam al-Lubnaniya*. pp. 24–25.

31. The behaviour of Lebanese women of the emerging comprador bourgeoisie was an act of propaganda for the WCS, and especially French companies. They were the internal basis for the changing tastes, culture, and habits. For example, while the import of perfume between 1924 and 1930 increased 400%, the import of industrial machinery increased by only 30%, Massoud Daher, op. cit., p. 115.

32. Abdallah Bouhabib, *New Frontiers in American Lebanese Relations*, Center for International Development, University of Maryland, 1984, pp. 6–7.

33. Samih Farsoun, *Merip Reports*, Dec., 197?, p. 5.

34. Dubar and Nasr, op. cit., p. 72.

35. Ibid., p. 69.

36. Salim Nasr, op. cit., p. 4.

37. Samih Farsoun, op. cit., p. 5.

38. *Middle East Economic Digest* (Sec. 27, 1974). p. 1590.

39. M. Chamie 'Labor Force Participation of Lebanese Women', in *Employment and Development*, ed. J. Abu Nasr, N. Khoury, H. Azzam, p. 81.

40. Ibid., p. 81.

41. S. Farsoun and K. Farsoun, 'Class and Patterns of Association Among Kinsmen in Contemporry Lebanon', *Anthropological Quarterly*, Vol. 47, p. 94.

42. Chamie, op. cit., p. 81.

42. Farsoun and Farsoun, op. cit., p. 95. (*N.B. second Notes number 42. EMS*)

43. Chamie, op. cit., p. 76.

44. Irene Lorfing, 'Women Workers in the Lebanese Industry', Paper submitted to *Institute for Women's Studies in the Arab World*, Beirut University College, March 1983, p. 1.

45. Women in the capitalist system do the jobs that are marginal to the mode of production that can, in most cases, be replaced by machines in a more developed stage of capitalism. Also they do not own the means of production. So their relation to the mode of production, especially in the case of underdeveloped capitalism, is continuously marginalized and peripheralized. They constitute the 'reserve cheap labour force'.

46. Irene Lorfing, M. Chamie and Farsoun in the articles previously mentioned; also R. Tabbara in 'Population, Human Resources and Development in the Arab World', *Population Bulletin of ECWA*; S. Nasr and M. Nasr in 'Les Travailleurs de la Grande Industrie, dans la Banlieu et de Beyrouth' (unpublished), and K. Khalaf in *Beirut Urbanization and Hamra*, and *Prostitution in Changing Society*, 1975. All emphasized the effects of urbanization; each has his/her own approach. Some see the positive aspect of modernization while they could not deny the negative side of these effects on women; others, especially Farsoun and Nasr, pointed out the effects of capitalist development which benefits the very few over the suffering of the very many, of whom women are particularly affected.

47. Lorfing, op. cit., p. 3.

48. Nasr and Nasr, 'Les Travailleurs de la Grande Industrie, dans la Banlieu et de Beyrouth'. 1974. Beirut (unpublished). Nasr's book *Les Classes Sociales au Liban*. reflects a similar thesis.

49. Lorfing, op. cit., p. 3.

50. Chamie, op. cit., pp. 77–95.

51. Lorfing, op. cit., p. 4.

52. Ibid., p. 5.

53. Chamie, op. cit., p. 81.

54. Farsoun and Farsoun, op. cit., pp. 93–107.

55. Suad Joseph, op. cit., pp. 1–3.

56. Farsoun and Farsoun, op. cit., p. 95.

57. Marie Aziz Sabri, *Pioneering Profiles. Beirut College for Women*, Beirut, 1967, pp. 18–19.

58. Lorfing, op. cit., p. 11.

59. Najla Bachour, *Lebanese Women*, Beirut, 1975, p. 22.

13. The Role of Alienation and Exploitation of Women in the Origins of State and Capitalism in the Sudan

Fatima Babiker Mahmoud

This chapter aims to describe the position of slave women during the Funj Sultanate in Sudan (1500–1821), and begins with an account of the political economy of the Sultanate. My analysis departs from those of scholars who adopted Samir Amin's theory that the tributary mode of production dominated during that period. I shall, instead, argue that the Funj economy was dominated by the slave mode of production.

In the second part of this chapter the relationship between the Funj State and the growing mercantile class and the reproduction of the Funj system is explained. In order for the Sultan to ensure his control over the state, continue slave raids and eliminate the merchant class' competition for political power, slave women were forced to sell their bodies within a system of institutionalized sexual exploitation. The Sultan's objectives were: first to supply the army and the merchants along trade routes with sexual services; secondly, to supply the Sultanate army with soldiers since slave women's children were taken and reared by the state, and then recruited into the army; and thirdly, to provide the state machinery with administrators in order to ensure that no ethnic groups other than those who already monopolized the state competed for political power.

The Sultanate period saw the origin of the first despotic Sudanese state and the beginnings of the development of a merchant class. This chapter attempts to establish that the enslavement and exploitation of women played a crucial role in consolidating the state and in early capital accumulation, both by the state and the embryonic merchant capitalist class.

Literature on the Funj and women

Literature published on the Funj may be divided into three categories. The first, written by historians and travellers (Arkel, Spandling, Ofaley, Terry Abu Salim and others) is rich and useful, but generally descriptive and gender and/or class blind. The second, written during the last decade by a few Sudanese scholars departed from a political economy focus and, although it discussed the Funj society as a class society (Sid Ahmed 1982; Shad Aldin 1981; M. A. Karim 1984), it also suffered from gender blindness. The third category is that written by Sudanese feminists. One such study (Haga Kashif 1981) failed to see the clear nature of gender in differences in Funj society and consequently completely disregarded the incidence of exploitation with which this chapter is concerned. Haga Kashif described the Funj economy in the following terms: 'The Funj organization was based on a feudal tribal system with some elements which characterize what the economists refer to as the subsistence traditional economy.' Moreover Haga stated that:

> Slavery during that period and in Sudan generally provided protection for all members of the tribe including slaves. Slavery in Sudan was more human if compared to slavery in Europe. The master in Sudan represented a father or an elder brother. Moreover, some masters married their female slaves and allowed female slave children to inherit their property.[1]

Scholars writing about the Funj Sultanate within a political economy perspective focused on almost every aspect of political economy except that concerning women. This perhaps explains why they failed to focus on the sexual exploitation of female slaves as one of the important factors in the process of merchants' accumulation of wealth.

In discussing the political economy of the Funj, Sid Ahmed and Shaa' Aldin adopted Samir Amin's model and argued that the tributary mode of production predominated during the Funj Sultanate (Sid Ahmed 1982; Shaa' Aldin 1980).

Samir Amin stated that:

> The Asiatic mode of production [which he called tributary] is very close to the feudal mode of production. It is characterized by the organization of society into two main classes: the peasantry, organized into communities and the ruling class, which monopolizes the society functions of political organization and levies tribute from rural communities.[2]

This model of the tributary mode of production is problematic in that it leans heavily upon how production is organized rather than how production is materially realized. There are a number of other reasons why this model is inappropriate when applied to the Funj economy. Firstly, the two main classes in the Funj were not the peasantry and the ruling class. There were the masters: comprising the ruling dynasty, the merchants, some rich peasants in the riverian lands, and the religious men and tribal chiefs, none of whom contributed to material production but they did have access to the surplus. The producers within the Funj economy included agricultural and nomadic communal groups as well as slaves, with slave production providing the most significant share of the total output; production organized within communal relationships was largely devoted to consumption. Co-operative production was also practised in the riverain lands of the Funj. The political economy of the Funj also witnessed an embryonic form of feudal production especially during the second half of the Sultanate. Based on these observations it is difficult to classify the Funj economy as one in which the 'tributary mode' of production predominated.

The Funj: climate and conditions

The Funj Sultanate was situated in the Nile Valley between Egypt, the Abyssinian highlands and the swamps of Nilotic Sudan.[3] It was an area of vast plains, interspersed with a few widely separated groups of hills and mountains. Divided from south to north by the river Nile and its affluents[4] it exhibited two distinct climatic zones. One, the immense desert region located north of Aldamar, with a yearly rainfall of between 20mm and 25mm, supported poor vegetation concentrated mainly in empty water courses; the population was consequently forced to the banks of the Nile. Where the valley was narrow only a small sedentary population could make a living, but at Dongola the river broadened and thus enabled a large population to exist. To the east and west of the Nile were nomadic tribes. The second climatic zone was the savannah, which stretched south of al-Damar to include the southern and central parts of the Sultanate. Here rainfall increased progressively until it reached 600mm annually in the extreme south.

Social labour, especially during the first decade, was almost wholly devoted to the production of foods. The social surplus product was small, particularly within the nomadic and subsistence agriculture sectors. The Sultan of Sinnar had unlimited rights over the natural resources of the kingdom and the material possessions of his subjects;[5] in addition he had the right to confiscate any land in the Sultanate and to impose tax in all lands.

Communal ownership and the emergence of a master's/quasi feudal class in the riverain area

Communal ownership existed in the riverain lands amongst shifting agriculturalists and nomads: labour is a decisive factor in shifting cultivation while the most crucial factor for nomads is land.[6] The organization of production is based on the family as a unit of production and the tribe as the owner of land. The right to the ownership of land was devolved directly from the Sultan through his provincial rulers. Land was given into the ownership of the tribal chief, while members of the tribe had equal rights in its use.[7] It lay within the power of the chief to allot land among the members of the tribe, settle tribal disputes and rent cultivable land to strangers. The tribal chief was expected to bring as much land as possible under cultivation, and to this end emigrants were allowed to cultivate land in return for rent or there was extensive exploitation of slaves.

The tribal chief's reward for his services was the right to own private land and to exploit the wild life within his tribal territory. Under the then existing tribal structure the Funj government administrative policy provided the necessary conditions for the emergence of classes in the riverain areas of Sudan. Sheikhs manifested a dual class character; on the one hand they were organizing a quasi feudal form of production by renting lands to emigrants, and on the other they reinforced the then existing slave relation by their intensive utilization of slave labour to increase the area of cultivable land.

Thus, the first class division within the communal form of production in the nomadic and agriculturalist Funj Sultanate was as a result of the state's political discrimination rather than of an internal contradiction within the communal form.

Individual ownership

Those members of the Sultanate who were given the right to private property were state administrators, as well as holy men who represented an important ideological group in maintaining the system. Thus the representatives of the classes that emerged from the communual form of organization of production were state functionaries and ideologists.

Individual land ownership in these areas had been established long before the Christian kingdoms had collapsed and been replaced by the Funj Sultanate.[8] Farmers who owned this type of land accumulated wealth through utilization of the existing techniques of production; those who owned more than one waterwheel were able to cultivate vast areas.[9] Depending on the type of labour employed in this process, feudal and/or slave exploitation was realized.

Co-operative land ownership was based on the collective ownership of a waterwheel either by six or eight semi-poor families or by extended families who could not afford to acquire individual waterwheels of their own. The collective consequently enjoyed full land ownership rights. Co-operative ownership was also dictated by the shortage of land and underdeveloped production techniques.

The Funj population

Historians' accounts and travellers' notes are the main source of data on the Funj population; a modern classified account is, therefore, not possible. We do not know, for example, the number of females in the Funj society, or nomadic and agricultural producers.

Taken as a whole the Funj Sultanate was sparsely populated, especially in the desert and steppe region. The fertile riverain and southern districts were more thickly populated but never densely.[10] The number of the inhabitants has, however, been estimated to have averaged approximately 200,000.[11]

Generally speaking the Funj population falls into two major classes: first a productive majority which included free agriculturalists, pastoralist tribesmen and slaves; and secondly, an unproductive minority composed of the ruling dynasty, that is, the Funj Sultan and his family, tribal chiefs, holy men and wealthy merchants. According to Burkhardt, the number of slaves during the Funj Sultanate was never fewer than 12,000, and this figure covers only the Nile valley, between Berber and Sinnar, which is approximately one-fourth of the Funj area.

A distinction could possibly be made between the slave and non-slave population on the basis of age; the elderly and children were unlikely to be captured. Raiders would single out strong, young slaves who could be utilized either in material production or sold. Female domestic slave labour probably replaced a considerable proportion of ruling class females' production in this area.

The literature on the Funj (including that arguing along the lines of the predominance of a tributary mode of production) suggests that slave participation in material production was the most fundamental aspect of the process of capital accumulation. This was not due to the number of slaves (there were obviously fewer than free people), but rather on the type of production in which they were engaged, and its importance to trade and consumption.

Sid Ahmed, who classified the Funj political economy as characterized by the predominance of the tributary mode of production, wrote:

> Furthermore, one cannot say that the Sultan engaged in trade simply on the basis of tribute collection. Indeed it was *slave labour* that produced most of the export commodities of the royal trade. The slaves themselves were an important item in the export (Walz 1978). Moreover, they were in the procurement of other commodities. They cultivated land, worked the gold mines, collected ivory, tended forests and collected gum in addition to the processing and manufacturing of skins and cotton.[12]

Slave labour was used not only to cultivate the royal land but also the privately owned riverain estates of merchants and holy men, and even on communally owned land. In organizing production on behalf of the tribe, tribal leaders engaged in extensive exploitation of slave labour.

It could be argued that the population engaged in subsistence production. The majority of the Funj population produced mainly for consumption. The tributes appropriated from them were not significant compared to that appropriated from the wealthy who extensively used slave labour.

J. C. Burkhardt stated 'that the slaves of both sexes on the border of the Nile from Berber to Sennar. [were] not less than 12,000'. He added that a minimum of 1,000 slaves was bought annually by the Danaqula and Bedouin who lived to the east of Shendy towards Atbara and the Red Sea. Slaves were captured from the pagan territories to the south of Sinnar, that is, Fazoogli, the Shilluk country, the Nouba mountains for example. Thus it was an established practice that each year a Sultan-sponsored slave raid (*ghazwa*), was organized by a special court official known as Mugaddam al-Salatin. Half the captured slaves were claimed by the Funj Sultan; the men were immediately incorporated in the army, the women taken into the harem as concubines, and very few joined the bureaucracy. The rest were exported along with other articles of the royal trade, the number in this category was estimated as between 2,000 to 3,000 annually.[13] In other words, more than half the captured slaves were destined for the army and as commodities for the royal trade. Moreover, and in order to ensure the political support of the wealthy the Sultan made slave grants for holy men, tribal chiefs and so on. To borrow Spandling and O'Fahey's description:

Slaves were kept in large numbers by the Sultan, Mekks, Manjils, wealthy merchants, tribal chiefs and later in the 19th century, by holymen. They were exploited in ways such as the cultivation of land, tending of cattle, domestic and military services.

Calliand stated that,

Some of them make cloth of their cotton, and worked themselves in the fields. Those who enjoy a measure of wealth, employ slaves of both sexes for the latter work and devote themselves entirely to commerce.[14]

Clearly it is evident that slaves were a very important class, not only as agricultural and artisanal producers, but also in so far as: 1) ensuring the reproduction of the Sultanate army; 2) buying the support of important ideological groups of holy men, as well as merchants, governors and tribal leaders; and 3) as a class that belonged to no group competing for political power, but rather acting as a buffer to prevent competition between potentially powerful groups.

The Funj women

Subjection, alienation and exploitation of women in the Funj Sultanate was essentially class determined. There were, 1) the mistresses; 2) free women; 3) slaves.

The mistresses

These were the wives of the ruling dynasty, of merchants and holy men, and – especially in the riverain lands since the second century of the Sultanate – rich peasants.

Slave women were exploited by mistresses in the domestic sphere as well as for making pottery and weaving. Compared to their non-producing husbands, however, mistresses were responsible for producing children as well as entertaining their husbands. Slave women were also required to massage both masters and wives, and to attend to the mistresses' toilet – preparing perfumes, dressing their hair – and to entertain them when they were bored.

Bruce's description of Sinnar mistresses and the slave women (a Sinnar sheikh [Regional Governor] asked him to examine some of his wives who were ill) was as follows:

In an alcove sat one of his wives . . . with a number of black slaves about her . . . the Sheikh brought a second wife from another apartment, and set her down beside the first one. They were both women past middle age, and seemed to have a great many slaves attending them.

Bruce went on to describe how the slaves were treated:[15] he asked the sheikh to send them away so that he could examine the mistresses and noted that the sheikh . . . 'did not seem at a loss how to do this, for he took up a short whip, or switch which lay at hand, and happy were they who got first to the door.'[16] Of one of the sheikh's wives, Bruce had the following to say:

> Her hair [was] long, and in great quantity . . . braided and twisted round like a crown, ornamented with beads, and the white, common Guinea-shells, commonly known here by the name of blackmoor's teeth. She had plain rings and gold in her ears, and four rows of gold chains about her neck. Her whole features were faultless: they might have served alone for the study of a painter all his life.[17]

This portrait also tells us that not only was the sheikh permitted to marry several women but to take as wife a young girl below fifteen years old.

Free women
In nomadic and subsistence agriculture, women's contribution seems to have played the crucial part in total production. Women shared agricultural and nomadic production with men and in addition were responsible for domestic work as well as for artisanal production.

Female slaves: sexual exploitation and alienation
Sexual exploitation of women during the Funj was suffered by both slaves and free women. This particular form of exploitation is not mentioned in the published literature but it is of interest because of the important part it played in the reproduction of the Sultanate army and administration and especially in view of the role it played in the development of merchant capital.

Female slaves' sexual exploitation was associated with the development of long distance trade and the growth of towns in the Funj. Sinnar, Shendy and Berber were described as the most important towns and centres for trade but by the 18th and 19th centuries there were at least 20 commercial centres.[18] According to Calliand, wealthy merchants often set the female slaves to work as prostitutes in towns along the trade routes. The girls were allocated quarters and paid a fixed monthly fee out of their earnings by the master.[19] Spandling added that some noblemen, fearing competition from the merchants, adopted the same system.[20]

Historians and travellers referred to this form of exploitation as prostitution, but I would argue that it constituted sexual exploitation based on direct coercion and, therefore, cannot be classified as prostitution.

In addition to institutionalized sexual exploitation, Hoskin reported that, 'All illegitimate children, including those of free women, were considered slaves and the property of the King.' Consequently, according to Hoskins, the Melek (the king or sultan) always had a large force of slaves and dependants. Intercourse between women servants of the royal household and free men was also tolerated and even encouraged.[21] This raises certain issues in terms of both the process of merchant capital accumulation and reproduction of the system. These can be summarized as: 1) the nature of that particular form of sexual exploitation; 2) the fee offered to female slaves rendering sexual service; and 3) the Sultan's appropriation of slave women's offspring to maintain the army and to supply the system with loyal administrators.

This form of exploitation took place under total and direct coercion, and depended on particular physical characteristics, such as age and beauty. As Marx wrote, 'In the case of the slave, great physical strength or a special talent may enhance his value to a purchaser, but this is of no concern to him. It is otherwise with the free worker who is the owner of his labour power.' Sexually exploited female slaves are separated from their sexuality, they do not own their bodies which become an instrument of labour and like any instrument, in rendering their particular services, their body is subject to depreciation.

The business merchants were interested in: 1) providing sexual services to caravan travellers; and 2) accumulating profit and providing the army and the state administration with loyal personnel. The monthly cash payment the merchants gave to the women slaves, which Calliand called 'free', was not a wage in the strict meaning of the term, but part of the cost of reproduction of this particular slave group. The money was to buy ornaments, elegant clothes and perfume; in short, to enhance trade and thus improve the most important aspect of the business and increase or maintain its value. The special value of these females necessitated a special cost of reproduction.

For the purpose of reproducing the Funj state system slave females were separated from their body and from the fruit or perhaps the product of their labour, their offspring. I am not proposing a 'motherhood ideology' but I believe this form of exploitation to be alienating, since alienation of labour is not only alienation of the product of labour, but alienation of the form and contents of work itself.[22]

When the Funj female slaves became so old that their value decreased compared to their cost of reproduction they were forced out of this particular form of exploitation and put to work either in the master's household or fields. Most of them joined the household where they were engaged in beautifying the mistresses, or other personal services, such as massage of master and mistresses. Those who were still physically strong, however, were sold in the market along with the other articles of the merchant's trade.

Summary and conclusion

In this chapter I have argued that: 1) Samir Amin's model, when applied to the Funj, incorrectly emphasizes the level and organization of distribution rather than of production; 2) even if Amin's model is accepted, the political economy of the Funj Sultanate did not provide the characteristics Amin prescribed for his tributary mode; 3) the early literature on the Funj Sultanate was both gender and class blind; 4) recent writing on the Funj political economy is also gender blind; 5) feminists who have tried to document the position of women during the Funj were class blind and as such failed to understand slavery as a form of exploitation, and consequently failed to perceive female sexual exploitation; 6) female exploitation during the Funj encompassed mistresses and free women, as well as female slaves; but the female slaves witnessed the most brutal forms of exploitation; 7) in addition to female exploitation, subordination and oppression during the Funj, female slaves who were chosen and coerced into sexual exploitation were subject to alienation.

Notes

1. Haga Kashif, 'The History of Sudanese Women's Movement', M.Sc. Thesis, Khartoum University, Khartoum, 1981. pp. 5–8.

2. Samir Amin, *Accumulation on a World Scale*, Monthly Review Press, New York, London, 1974, p. 140.

3. A. J. Arkel, 'The Historical Background in the Sudan', in Tothill, *Agriculture in the Sudan*, Oxford University Press, 1948, p. 17.

4. Spandling and O'Fahey, *Kingdoms of the Sudan*, London, Methuen, 1974, p. 1.

5. Ibid. p. 54.

6. J. Farmer. 'Herdsmen in Rainland Sennar'. *Journal of African History*. Vol. 20. No. 3. p. 37.

7. Ibid. p. 340.

8. Mohamed Ibrahim Abu Salim, *al-Ard Fi al-mahdiya*, Sudan Research Unit, Khartoum University, 1970, p. 10.

9. The riverain areas included both the *gerf* (land on the banks of the Nile) and *saqiyya* (a waterwheel driven by either human or animal labour).

10. J. P. Trimingham, *Islam in the Sudan*, London, Oxford University Press, 1949, p. 4.

11. Sayid Albushra, 'Towns in the Sudan in the Eighteenth Century', *Sudanese Notes and Records*, 1971, Vol. 52, p. 65.

12. Abdul Salam Sid Ahmed. 'The State and Islam in the Funj (1500–1821)'. M.Sc. thesis, University of Khartoum, 1983, p.63.

13. Spandling and O'Fahey, op. cit., p. 56.

14. Calliand, quoted in ibid. p. 81.

15. James Bruce, *Travels to Discover the Source of the Nile*, Edinburgh University Press, 1964, pp. 204–5.

16. Ibid. p. 205.

17. Ibid.

18. Alfatih Shaa' Aldin, 'The Process of Proletarization in the Sudan', Development Studies Research Centre, Khartoum, 1981, p. 6.

19. See Calliand, quoted in Spandling and O'Fahey, op. cit. p. 81.

20. Spandling and O'Fahey, op. cit. p. 56.

21. Quoted in ibid. p. 33.

22. 'The first way in which an object of utility attains the possibility of becoming an exchange value is to exist as a non-use-value superfluous to the immediate needs of its owner. Things are in themselves external to man and therefore alienate him.' Marx, *Capital*, Vol. 1, 1976, p. 182.

14. Arab Women's Solidarity Association (AWSA): Final Report and Recommendations

On the second day of the Conference (2 September 1986) delegates met to discuss position papers. After this meeting, participants constituted themselves into four committees: cultural, economic, political and social. On the following day each committee met and after electing their respective chairwoman and secretary relevant papers were carefully and intensively discussed before recommendations were finally drafted.

The final report was designed to incorporate the main topics of discussion as well as the committees' recommendations. There was general consensus on the various issues discussed, but specifically there was agreement that the dependence of Arab countries on world capitalism in all spheres – economic, cultural, political and social – underlies many problems of women in the Arab world and it is the effects of this dependence that present them with a great challenge. This state of affairs has tied the Third World to the capitalist world in terms of production, consumption and trade exchange, and marginalized women's economic role rendering the benefits reaped from social reproduction subject to the accumulation of local capital as an extension to world capital. It was agreed that the matter of dependency must be considered at domestic and international levels. Social classes involved in exploitation provide the link between the centre and the periphery and, in the interests of world capital – the local component as well as multinational corporations – facilitate the centre's exploitation of the periphery.

Culture is directed towards reinforcing the subordinate position of women by a process of increasing institutionalization eventually leading women themselves to adopt and internalize this subordinate role. National politics in Arab countries deliberately ignore the position of women. Laws are constantly enacted that directly or indirectly both usurp women's acquired rights and put an end to any possibility of progress in their struggle towards emancipation.

The dependency factor means that women are either isolated and their economic role usurped by inappropriate technology, or subject to increased burdens as a result of the growing gap in economic development between rural and urban areas which forces men to migrate to the cities, or even to other countries, in search of employment.

The four committees agreed on the need for vigorous efforts to raise public awareness of the issue of dependency in so far as it affects all spheres of life.

These efforts should be directed towards all social classes, with special emphasis on the exploiters; such awareness is primarily a social issue, as well as one of feminist concern. It was asserted that women themselves should lead their struggle for emancipation and not expect other social groups to fight their battles.

Recommendations

Political Committee
The Arab area, particularly in its political institutions, is still characterized by political dependence on former colonizers often in their new guise of neo-imperialism. These are the same capitalist systems that support Zionism and Israel in its occupation of Palestine, south Lebanon and other Arab countries, and in its persistent terrorist actions against the Arab countries.

Political decision in the Arab countries is by no means a decision of governments as a whole. These governments are characterized by a hierarchical system dependant on the rule of the individual and the monopolization of opinion by those afraid of plurality and freedom of thought. They pay lip service to the masses against whom they exercise repression; one of its forms, sexual oppression, is directed against women who represent 50% of these masses.

History has taught us that no repressed group may be liberated except by its own struggle and this applies to the case of women. We call for women to unite, to close ranks and become a political and social force able to effect changes in prevailing systems, laws and legislation that will be beneficial not only for women but for all the people.

The political committee made the following recommendations:

1. The solidarity of Arab women is the spearhead for mobilizing efforts to realize their emancipation and to succeed in fulfilling their goals. Arab women's solidarity may provide a model for the long desired attainment of Arab unity that is vitally necessary in order to resist those foreign and internal forces that usurp the Arab nation's right to freedom and independence. Without such unity, Arab governments will continue to accept submissive solutions to their problems, to conclude treaties that strip the Arab people of their dignity and strengthen their enemies. The masses of the Arab nation – men and women – are to this day still disunited and isolated. Only by all Arab peoples' commitment to unity and real independence can their ability to resist and attain victory be safeguarded.

2. We call for the release of general freedoms, particularly the freedoms of expression and organization; for respect of human rights for men and women; for a greater participation by women in political decision-making, and for an equal share with men in the authority exercised both in the state and the family.

3. We aim to raise awareness of the United Nations Covenant for the Elimination of All Forms of Discrimination Against Women and to urge Arab countries and organizations to sign, ratify and implement its provisions.

4. We call for martial laws, emergency laws and special tribunals in Arab countries to be abolished; respect for the independence of the judiciary to be fostered; and for the principle of the separation of powers to be upheld.

5. We aim to search all texts in Arab legislation that discriminate against women by analysing and explaining their implications; and to work towards their cancellation, modification or change, or the addition of new clauses to fill legal and procedural gaps.

6. We call on official and popular feminist organizations in the Arab countries to struggle for the enactment of a civil personal status code to be applied to all citizens without discrimination on the basis of sex or religious belief.

Economic Committee
The economic systems in the Arab world have been distorted by colonialism and by dependency on the economies of capitalist states.

Apart from the undesirability of moving in the orbits of the policies and objectives of these states, the dependency has decisively influenced the marginalization of women's economic role, which has led to their exploitation, the intensification of their oppression and alienation, and the negation of their role in production and reproduction.

Women's dependency under the capitalist system constitutes an integral cause of the subordination of women and the family in the patriarchal system. Domestic work, as unrecognized and unwaged labour, is a cornerstone of the capitalist system and the accumulation of capital.

The following recommendations were put forward by the Economic Committee:

Major recommendations

1. Links to the world capitalist system and dependence on its institutions should be identified as a major cause of the ongoing social and economic backwardness of the Arab world, of the dependency of Arab women, of their exploitation and the marginalization of their economic role in production and reproduction.

2. The need to adopt means for realizing overall, well-balanced, socio-economic development. By 'development' we mean the introduction of radical change to economic structures, the mobilization of human resources in particular and freeing the potentials of women and men, with the aim of increasing production and of maintaining equitable distribution of wealth.

3. The need to promote the participation of women in decision-making in the sphere of economics, and their greater representation in economic organizations as well as in such organizations as political parties, trade unions, and similar groups.

4. The need to encourage women to participate vigorously in the public control of commodities and in consumer protection by means of the

establishment of special associations or by undertaking political and economic actions, such as boycotts or demonstrations, which are efficient and effective, to procure satisfaction of their economic demands.

5. The need to re-evaluate women's unwaged domestic work and to include it as productive labour, for which material and moral remuneration, in proportion to its extent and its importance to society and the family, is owing.

6. The need to open all areas of employment and training to women, covering decision-making in the state, judicial positions, designing legislation, the army and other such areas so far exclusive to men.

7. The need to discourage the employment of women in activities related to their domestic role (embroidery, weaving, secretarial work, nursing, domestic help and so on).

Recommendations of a conceptual nature

1. Economic concepts derived from the actual reality and needs of the Arab society should be substituted for the adopted economic concepts derived from the capitalist economic model. For example, concepts related to labour, national product, economic activity and so on. Such reactionary Western economic concepts have been abandoned by many Western researchers, but are still employed as tools of research and analysis in Arab countries and serve only to exacerbate the absence of women's participation in economic activity in the Arab world.

2. Theoretical, practical and field research on the structure of dependency of the Arab countries and its impact on women should be intensified.

3. Field studies should be conducted in urban and rural areas, aimed at discovering the real needs of Arab women, to serve as inputs for overall, well-balanced socio-economic programmes. Special emphasis is placed on the need for studies that would contribute to the designing of economic plans to redress the current distortions in the socio-economic structure of Arab societies. For example, migration from rural to urban areas and the sharp discrepancies between the two areas in developmental terms that are primarily responsible for the victimization of women.

Raising awareness

1. Raising awareness of the role played by the media in propagating dependency, particularly cultural dependency. This role distorts values and inhibits independent thinking by women and particularly by children, perpetuates the values of consuming and encourages the desire for ever more consumption, thus ultimately serving the increased entrenchment of dependency.

2. Raising the awareness of consumers, particularly women, of the significance of certain commodities and their role in terms of capitalist exploitation, and calling women's attention to the need to support local products and to resist the attraction of goods for which, in the long term, women may pay for manifold in terms of their economic and sexual exploitation.

Social Committee

Social problems confronting Arab women, long classified as individual and personal, are none other than the natural product of the social composition of the patriarchal extended family system in an economy dependent on capitalism with all its cultural implications. Such a system imposes limitations on little girls as well as on adult women, stunting their growth, stifling their potentials and restraining their full self-realization. Arab women are unaware of the true causes underlying their social backwardness and of the fact that it is the absence of democracy that hinders them forming organizations capable of raising and propagating awareness. These are the basic impediments to their conceptual development and to the development of their struggle in a manner conducive to the creation of a legal and cultural environment favourable to the realization of change.

Following are recommendations by the Social Committee:

1. To call for women's right to form free associations by calling for the institution of democracy and the freedom of expression for all Arab peoples.

2. To work intensively within political and popular organizations to put greater emphasis on women's issues from a feminist perspective.

3. To call for the allocation of funds for relevant organizations to conduct research and studies concerning Arab women's fundamental problems in order to collect data and information on the conditions of women.

4. To emphasize the recommendations of the Conference on women held in Nairobi and to aim at the adoption and implementation of its resolutions by Arab governments.

5. To assert that waged labour is a fundamental human right incorporated in all international covenants and in the Declaration of Human Rights, for women and men equally, and that this right should not be subjected to any political balances or conflicts between different economic forces; that it is a right that must not be relinquished.

6. To give special attention to curriculae taught to children in order to eliminate all elements that discriminate between men and women with regard to their rights and duties, or the division of labour within or outside the home, on the basis of sex. To create educational material which promotes the values of equality between the sexes in potentials, unrestrained development of abilities, and to disrupt social stereotypes. This will encourage the development of a young generation free of sex discrimination and prejudices and unleash their creative energy.

7. To give attention to the issues of divorced women and to women victimized by social repression, and to find alternative means for them to survive and confront social injustice.

8. To organize a voluntary fund for the Women's Solidarity Association in the Arab world.

9. To seek to link people's health problems in general with social conditions, particularly the psychological and physical problems of women, conducting studies to reveal the relation between health problems and social conditions;

furthermore, to raise the awareness of health personnel – at the various levels – of the overall meaning of health, dissuading them from reliance on imported methods of treatment and on drugs inappropriate to local conditions.

10. To assert that motherhood is the highest form of production, and a social function for which the state should provide the optimum opportunities and support; to stress that child-rearing is the joint responsibility of both parents and that this should be taken into consideration in the determination of work and time off for both partners and the establishment of work conditions conducive to this sharing of responsibility.

11. To establish relations with organizations of Arab women in migration, and to support women's struggle against racial, cultural or sex persecution in these societies.

Cultural Committee

Cultural research highlighted the fact that Arab countries are victims of cultural dependency to the extent that Arab culture has become a minuscule and deformed replica of Western culture. This may clearly be observed not only in official cultural institutions, but in various forms of popular culture. Thus the situation of women oscillates between two cultural currents: 1) the European which obviously does not reflect the culture of Arab countries; and 2) the religious *salafi*, oriented to the past and drawing on the practices of ancestors, that likewise does not necessarily reflect the culture prevailing in Arab countries, particularly in relation to the status of women. Caught between the two currents, Arab women's status has been affected equally negatively by both. The contradiction between these two currents are given material form by the media: the image of the veiled woman in her isolation (in accordance with *salafi* cultural values); and the image of a naked woman in commerical advertisements.

The Committee also observed that Arab literature is dominated by men. All nouns in the written language, in creative literature and elsewhere, including official texts, are masculine.

As a result of its discussions and review of research, the Cultural Committee made the following recommendations:

1. The publication of a magazine to reflect Arab women's views on issues of social and national concern in order to meet the challenges confronting the Arab nation at this critical stage of its history. Such a publication would also be especially relevant today as women's rights are undergoing a set-back precipitated by the *salafi* trend which threatens to deprive them of the rights they have gained after years of struggle.

2. The establishment of a publishing house primarily for the publication of women's writings, as well as serious, problem-oriented research and literary works dealing with women, in addition to translations of writings about women, whether or not their authors are women.

3. The establishment of a committee emanating from the Conference modelled on the Human Rights Committee, to protect the freedoms of thought, writing, opinion and creativity.

Appendix 1

Statement by Arab Women's Solidarity Association to the UN International Conference of Women, Nairobi: 10–26 July 1985

We, women, members of the Arab Women's Solidarity Association declare:

1. That there can be no peace without justice, and no equality without justice and no development without justice.

2. That the international order which prevails in the world of today whether it be political, economic, military, informational or commercial has failed to give peace or equality or development to the overwhelming majority of people, and in particular to the peoples of the 'Third World' countries.

3. That those who suffer most whether in peace or in war as a result of the unjust international order are the women, for women are the weakest section of the population politically, economically and socially. They shoulder the double burden of work both outside the home and in it, shoulder two-thirds of the total human effort expended on our earth. They earn only one-third of the income paid in return for labour, and own only one-tenth of the total property existing in the world. They have almost no political organizations to defend their rights or to change the laws which govern their lives.

4. That a limited minority of countries and individuals control the means of production of science and technology, of human thought and interchange. They own the wealth and power. Their interests, which are organized in the system of neocolonialism and giant multinational corporations, drive them to plunder the natural wealth and exploit the human potential of the Arab countries and of other 'Third World' countries in Asia, Africa and South and Central America. They use all the means at their disposal to crush the resistance of the peoples in these areas of the world and to sow discord and conflicts among them. To this end they encourage and support racist movements such as World Zionism, the apartheid government of South Africa and the extremist religious movements which have grown visibly over the past decade; they incite reactionary governments and movements to cause internal strife, or to invade the territories of other peoples and occupy their lands. What is happening to the Arabs of Palestine, to the people of tiny Lebanon, to Namibia, Grenada and Nicaragua and to many other countries of the world are examples.

5. That women are the first and the most vulnerable victims of religious and racist extremism. They suffer most from the fanatical movements which under the guise of religion aim their attacks at social, political and cultural emancipation of the peoples of the 'Third World'. These movements serve the interests of neocolonialism, in a direct or indirect way. They disguise the real causes for the growing crisis in the world of today, by emphasizing the need for

a return to the puritanical morals of bygone days, where corruption and vice were hidden behind the veil and the rituals of fasting, worship and prayer, and behind a zeal vented on women and minorities wherever they may be.

6. We, therefore, call upon the participants in this Conference to unite in condemning all forms of religious, sexist and racist fanaticism, and in unmasking the forces and interests which manipulate them in order to break people's resistance from inside. We know that the so-called religious revival is aimed at holding back our struggle for democracy, social justice, peace and freedom for all peoples. We know that its consequences will fall upon women above all, and prevent the development of equal and healthy relations between men and women, and within the family whatever its form.

7. We call upon all governments, especially in the Arab countries to implement the provisions of the human rights charter and protocol agreements which followed upon it, to abolish all forms of discrimination based on sex, gender and class, and to remove all restrictions on exercise of human freedoms and rights to both men and women alike, whether political, economic or cultural.

8. The problems related to the station of women cannot be separated from the general struggle for economic, social and political progress. They institute an integral part of the general democratic process. True democracy will never exist as long as women are deprived of equal rights.

True justice is not only an equal distribution of wealth. It necessarily implies an equal distribution of power within the state and within the family, the right of women to the proceeds of their physical and mental labour, and an equal right of decision for women as well as men within the family unit, and inside all institutions and organizations of the state.

Appendix 2

Arab Women's Solidarity Association (AWSA) Constitution

Preamble

The Arab Women's Solidarity Association is an Organization comprising representatives of women from the various Arab countries. It is an international non-governmental, non-profitable organization. It aims at promoting increasing awareness of Arab women's rights, defending these rights and mobilizing Arab women and men to develop them further. It seeks to organize women into an effective political power, thus enabling them to participate fully in the struggle of the Arab people for national independence, development, democracy and unity.

The establishment of AWSA is a response to the urgent need for emancipating the 'Arab mind' and liberating the Arab individual whether man or woman. This will pave the way to the evolution of a better Arab society based on justice, liberty and enlightened thought. It will also help in the mobilization of the human forces required to overcome discrimination, intolerance, backwardness and violence and in effectively combating the forces of new colonialism as well as the retrograde, fanatical religious movements seeking to turn back the clock of history for Arab women, and for the Arab peoples as a whole.

The contribution now being made by Arab women and by the AWSA has been carried out by many women pioneers since the earliest days. Building on this tradition, women throughout the Arab world, whether in urban or rural areas should insist on participating actively in solving the political, social and cultural problems which face our society. Foremost amongst the issues which face us today is that of independent, economic, social and cultural development in the face of foreign invasion, penetration and exploitation. It is only by struggling as a united force that people, both women and men, can hope to advance towards a brighter future.

SECTION ONE: Principles Guiding the Activities of AWSA and its Objectives

Article 1
1. Active participation of women in the political, economic and cultural reconstruction of Arab society. This active participation is a corner stone in

any true democracy, since it will permit women to achieve the political power which legitimately should be theirs as a force representing half the population of Arab society.

2. Social justice for women both in society and within the family. The abolition of discrimination on the basis of sex in both public and private life. Equitable distribution of power.

3. Development of the authentic personality of Arab women and their critical capacities. This will permit them to adopt a positive attitude towards their history and to realize the necessity for interaction between their traditional heritage and modern scientific thought.

4. Involvement of women in both urban and rural areas in the activities of the Association to ensure that it does not become an isolated elitist body, and that it maintains close contact with the problems and struggles of women belonging to the different classes and professions of society. Thus can be created the crucial link beteen Arab feminist theory and practice.

5. Forging even closer ties with Arab women in different Arab countries, as well as with women from the countries all over the world.

6. Opening the right to membership of the Association to men as well as women, with the aim of recruiting Arab men and youth who not only believe in the reconstruction of Arab society but also insist that such a reconstruction cannot be achieved without the birth of a new Arab woman capable of participating effectively in changing the life of the Arab peoples; men and youth who believe that the liberation of the Arab peoples cannot be achieved unless linked with the emancipation of Arab women.

Article II: Objectives of AWSA

1. To build up a front of solidarity between Arab women. The aims of this front are to mobilize women in defence of their rights and promote a growing awareness and understanding of these rights, to develop their sense of a national identity and of their independent personality, to instil a consciousness of their role in the reconstruction of Arab society, and of the need to struggle for Arab unity, social justice and democracy, as well as for an independent comprehensive development of Arab society which would include both women and men.

2. Active participation of women in evolving and executing national policies and plans aiming at the enhancement of the status and role of women in society and within the family, and the full development of their capabilities in the political, economic, social and cultural fields. Opening up avenues through which they can increasingly express themselves both in thought and in action.

3. Participation in the eradication of illiteracy amongst women. Teaching illiterate women to read and write should be done in close linkage with the enhancement of their political, social and cultural consciousness.

4. Publishing the work of women in the scientific, artistic, literary and cultural fields. Establishment of a women's publishing house, and the publication of a magazine specializing in scientific and cultural questions related to women. Sponsoring talented women in the various branches of knowledge and assisting them in the pursuit of their studies, their research work, or other fields of activity whether productive, artistic, or scientific.

5. The establishment of libraries comprising both old and more recent writings related to issues concerning women in the Arab countries and all over the world.

6. Undertaking field studies and applied research on working women in urban and rural areas. These studies will be published as a way of assisting those involved in women's studies or concerned with questions related to women in finding solutions to their problems. Establishing teams of women specialists which will undertake studies and research work in the various domains related to women.

7. The production of literary and dramatic works for radio, television, cinema and theatre as well as in the plastic arts whenever they are linked to women's problems, activities and aspirations.

8. Organization of regional and international conferences and seminars as a means for exchanging knowledge and experience between women.

SECTION TWO: Membership, Branches and Organization of AWSA

Article III
Membership of the Association is divided into three categories: active, associate, and honorary.

1. Any Arab woman (or man) who joins the Association, and pays the subscription with regularity is eligible for active membership and is entitled to stand for election to the General Assembly, the Board of Association and its Executive Committee.

2. Associate membership is accorded to any woman (or man) who applies for associate membership and pays the subscription regularly. Such members cannot vote or stand for election to the General Assembly, the Board of the Association or its Executive Committee.

3. Honorary membership is accorded to women (or men) who play a prominent role in activities related to women. Such membership is granted by decision of the Executive Committee subject to the approval of the Board of the Association. Payment of subscriptions by honorary members is optional. Such members are not entitled to nomination or election to the General Assembly, the Board or the Executive Committee.

4. Minimum age for membership is 15 years.

Article IV
Branches may be established in countries where there is an adequate number of members. External offices may also be established in non-Arab cities and capitals.

SECTION THREE: The Association's Organizational Structure

Article V
The Association's structure includes: The General Assembly, the Board and the Executive Committee. A general secretary, who should be a woman and preferably a full-timer, carries out the daily work of the Association. She is assisted by two appointed women members of the Association.

The General Assembly

Article VI
The General Assembly is the Association's highest authority. It decides on policies, monitors its activities and takes appropriate decisions for the development of the Association and its activities within the guidelines laid down by the Constitution.

Article VII
The General Assembly consist of:
1. Women members of the Board;
2. Women representatives of regional branches and women representatives of members in Arab countries where branches have not yet been set up as well as women representatives of offices in non-Arab countries, capitals and cities. After adoption of this constitution procedures of representation will be defined.

The Board may invite representatives of women's organizations and institutions or those concerned with women's affairs to attend meetings as observers. Prominent figures and those who play an important role in this field may also be invited.

Article VIII
The General Assembly holds its regular session once every three years on convocation by the Board. At the beginning of each session, a Chairwoman and a woman Rapporteur are elected.

If an urgent necessity arises, the General Assembly may be called upon to hold an extraordinary session on proposal of the Chairwoman of the Association if approved by a majority of the Board. An Extraordinary Session of the General Assembly may also be convened by one third of the members of the General Assembly subject to approval by one third of the members of the Board.

The Board

Article IX
The Board is responsible for the activities of the Association between the sessions of the General Assembly. The Board defines the policies of the Association within the guidelines laid down by the General Assembly and takes decisions for their execution and for supervising the activities of the various bodies of the Association.

Article X
The Board is composed of 15 members, elected by the General Assembly at a regular session held once every three years. The principle of geographical distribution should, as far as possible, be adhered to when selecting members of the Board.

Article XI
The Board meets at least once a year. The Chairwoman may call for the convocation of an extraordinary meeting in case of necessity.

The Executive Committee

Article XII
The Board elects an Executive Committee composed of four members:
1. The Chairwoman;
2. The Vice-Chairwoman;
3. The General-Secretary; and
4. The Treasurer.

The Executive Committee carries out the daily work of the Association in between the meetings of the Board. Its members are, therefore, required to be living in the country whe e the Headquarters of the Association are based.

Article XIII
The Executive Committee is empowered to establish its technical and administrative structure, and to draw up the rules governing the employment and salaries of those appointed.

The specialized organs

Article XIV
A number of specialized organs and committees will be created by the Association. The formation of such organs and committees and their jurisdiction will be decided upon by the Executive Committee. Among those organs: The Women's Publishing House and the Magazine. Decisions on the setting up of such organs and committees should be subsequently submitted to the earliest meeting held by the Board.

SECTION FOUR: The Association's Rules of Procedure

Article XV
The Executive Committee will promulgate the required rules and regulations of procedure for the execution of the provisions of the Constitution. These rules will be subsequently referred for adoption, at the earliest subsequent meeting of the Board.

SECTION FIVE: Finances of the Association

Article XVI
The funds of the Association consist of:
1. Annual subscriptions of members and associate members.
2. Donations offered by individuals or institutions the aims of which are not incompatible with those of the Association. Such donations should be unconditional.
3. Any other resources derived from the activities of the Association.

Article XVII
The Executive Committee is empowered to draw up the financial and administrative rules of the Association.

SECTION SIX: Concluding Provisions

Article XVIII
This Constitution may be amended by a decision adopted by a two-thirds majority of the female members of the General Assembly on proposal by the Board of Governors.

Article XIX
The Headquarters of the Association are in Cairo. If unforeseen circumstances arise, the Board of Governors is empowered to select temporary Headquarters in any other Arab country.

The Arab Women's Solidarity Association has Consultative Status, Category II, with the United Nations Economic and Social Council.

Its headquarters are situated at: 25 Murad Street, Giza, Egypt.

Notes on Contributors

Rima Sabban: Lebanese journalist and activist. She has a master's degree in political science from Georgetown University, USA.

Iqbal Baraka: Well-known journalist and writer in popular Egyptian journals, in which her views on women's issues reach a large audience.

Fatima El Mernissi: Lecturer in sociology, Institute of Social Research, King Muhammad, al-Khamis University, Rabat, Morocco. Author of many feminist books in Arabic and French.

Nawal El Saadawi: Egyptian doctor, internationally known novelist, militant writer, speaker and campaigner on women's problems and their struggle for liberation; President of the Arab Women's Solidarity Society.

Mirvat El Tillawi: Egyptian diplomat; was Egypt's representative to the UN: represented Egypt at the 1985 Nairobi Conference on Women, as head of the official delegation. Played a critical role in drafting the document of the group of 77 ultimately adopted as the official declaration of the conference. Currently Egypt's Ambassador to Austria.

Rita Giacaman: Lecturer at the Community Health Unit, Bir Zeit University, Ramalla (West Bank). Active in organizing health workers to meet health needs in villages in the occupied lands.

Mai Haddad: Lebanese; graduated in medicine from the Arab University, Beirut; has an MSc in community medicine and works as a freelance regional consultant on primary health care. Currently consultant to Save the Children (WSA) in Lebanon and Sudan.

Fatima Babiker Mahmoud: Assistant Professor of Economics, University of Khartoum; active member of the Sudanese Writers' Union. Of her many publications, best known in English is *The Sudanese Bourgeoisie* (Zed Press, 1982).

Mona Odeh: Lecturer at the Community Health Unit, Bir Zeit University, West Bank. Active in organizing health workers to meet health needs in villages in the occupied lands.

Mona Rishmawi: Graduate of the Law Faculty, Cairo University. Palestinian, lives in the West Bank and works on the only human rights documentation centre in the country: *El Haq* (law in the service of man). Currently establishing a programme on legal literacy and legal services for Palestinian women.

Thaira A. Shaalan: Researcher at the National Centre for Research and Studies,

Sanaa, North Yemen. Currently in Paris, working on a doctoral thesis on women's labour in Yemen.

Mouinne Chelhi: Lecturer in psychology, Faculty of Medicine, Sousa University, Tunis.

Nahid Toubia: Sudanese doctor, graduated from Cairo University: has a specialization in surgery from the Royal College of Surgeons, UK. Author of many papers in Arabic and English on women's social and health issues, particularly female circumcision.

Dr Fuad Zakaria: Professor, Faculty of Arts, Cairo University. Well known religious thinker and philosopher; modern interpreter of Islam. In the past few years he has opposed the tide of fundamentalism threatening to overtake Egypt and the Arab world. Author of several publications in Arabic.

Index

OCT 2 '90 APR 0 4 2002			
SEP 21 1995			
DEC 0 5 1996			
APR 2 1 1998			
MAR 1 3 2000			
APR 0 4 2000			
JUN 0 7 2001			
JUN 1 8 2001			
JUN 2 7 2001			
DEC 1 2 2001			